99
MY LIFE IN PICTURES

WAYNE GRETZKY
WITH JOHN DAVIDSON

EDITED BY DAN DIAMOND

A
Dan Diamond and Associates
Mint Publishers
Book

TOTAL SPORTS
CANADA

Official Publication

Published in Canada by:
Total Sports Canada
194 Dovercourt Road
Toronto, Ontario M6J 3C8
Canada
e-mail: dda.nhl@sympatico.ca

Published in the United States by:
Total Sports Publishing Inc.
100 Enterprise Drive
Kingston, NY 12401

Trade sales in Canada by:
Publishers Group West
250 Carlton Street
Toronto, Ontario M5A 2L1
Canada

Distribution in Canada by:
Canbook Distribution Services
1220 Nicholson Road
Newmarket, Ontario L3Y 7V1
Canada

Trade sales and distribution in the United States by:
Publishers Group West
1700 Fourth Street
Berkeley, CA 94710

Total Sports Canada books may be purchased for
educational, business or sales promotional use.
For information please write to:
Total Sports Canada
194 Dovercourt Road
Toronto, Ontario M6J 3C8
Canada
e-mail: dda.nhl@sympatico.ca

Permissions appear on page 223.

A conscientious attempt has been made to contact
proprietors of the rights in every image used in the
book. If through inadvertence the publisher has failed to
identify any holder of rights, forgiveness is requested and
corrected information will be entered in future printings.

Total Sports Canada™ is a trademark of Total Sports Inc. used under license.

Licensed by the National Hockey League®

Managing Editor: Eric Zweig
Senior Writer: Stu Hackel
Copy Editor: David Kilgour
Photo Research: Ralph Dinger
Statistics: James Duplacey
Project Management and Design: Dan Diamond

Library of Congress Catalog Card Number: 99-66171

ISBN 1-892129-19-1

Printed by World Color, Versailles, Kentucky
Scanning, Color Correction and Electronic Prepress by Stafford Graphics, Toronto

Printed in the United States of America

10 9 8 7 6 5 4 3 2 1

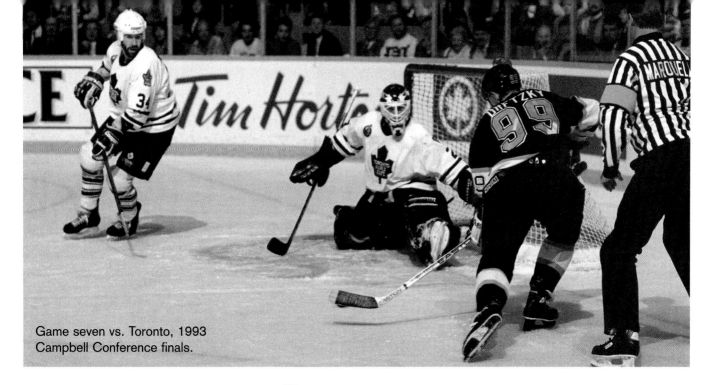

Game seven vs. Toronto, 1993
Campbell Conference finals.

Contents

Wayne Gretzky was selected Most Valuable Player at the 1999 NHL All-Star Game in Tampa, Florida. This was his league-leading fourth All-Star MVP award.

Foreward

I HAVE HAD THE PLEASURE OF PUBLISHING BOOKS ABOUT HOCKEY since 1984 when I redesigned the *NHL Official Guide & Record Book*. At that time, Wayne Gretzky was a five-year NHL veteran, a five-time NHL most valuable player, a five-time NHL All-Star and the league's only 200-point single-season scorer. The first cover I produced featured a photograph of him gazing up, admiring his reflection in the Stanley Cup. This would prove to be a lasting image, as Gretzky and his Oilers would win three more Stanley Cup titles in the next four seasons.

Through all of this, as the points, awards, records, accolades and years piled up, I frequently would find myself peering through a magnifying glass, looking at more and more pictures of the Great One. Throughout the 1980s and into the 1990s, he was hockey's ultimate front cover icon. His numbers and accomplishments were irrefutable. You lead with your best, and he was hockey's.

I came to see my magnified relationship with Wayne as a metaphor about sports and celebrity: here was one person who did his job so well that someone he had never met would have reason to put him under a microscope so that others could savor what he had accomplished. But what set Wayne apart from the standard celebrity model was this: the closer you looked, the more you knew you were dealing with a real person who just happened to be the world's greatest hockey player.

Now that he has retired after twenty seasons in the NHL, the opportunity exists to appreciate his career in both its breadth and depth. This book, *99: My Life In Pictures*, does that. More than 350 photographs—many never published before—sweep from novice hockey to the NHL and from son to father. The stories behind the images and observations about the game of hockey are provided by Wayne himself. His commentary begins on page 23, and each Gretzky entry is flagged "**99**."

Gretzky has also written an introduction which deals with how it feels to step away from that which defines you. See page ix.

John Davidson, a former NHL goaltender who now broadcasts New York Rangers hockey, writes "The Meaning of Wayne". This looks at Wayne's career in-depth, the forces that shaped him and his impact on the game in North America and throughout the world. See page 1.

A complete statistical panel is found on page 226.

Enjoy *99: My Life In Pictures*. Sports is a dangerous area in which to say "never," so I won't. Instead I propose the following: if another hockey player should come along whose on-ice achievements, personality and contribution to the game in any way match Wayne Gretzky's, point me to the ticket window. I want a pair at center ice from day one.

Dan Diamond
Toronto
August 1999

Making a tennis ball dance. Street hockey, 1978.

Introduction

U P UNTIL THE SECOND-LAST GAME of my final season, in Ottawa, I don't think my teammates really believed I was going to retire. I had a sort of ritual at the pre-game meal: I was the first guy in and the first guy out. Ten minutes. Bang-bang. It was a joke among my teammates because they knew I liked to keep to the same routine. But when we got to the pre-game meal in Ottawa, I could see that everybody was watching me from the corners of their eyes. We ended up sitting at that pre-game meal from 12:00 until 2:25. Nobody wanted to leave. We just sat around telling hockey stories, older guys asking the younger guys if they'd heard of this player or that player. I think it was then that everybody really knew I was going.

My last game, in New York, was the same way. When we got up on Sunday morning, my wife was more nervous than I was. A friend of hers had come over and my best friend from childhood had flown in from Columbus, Ohio. Other friends and family were there, and it was kind of crazy for an hour or so. And then I did what I had done for thirty years: I went to the game. I drove with my dad and his best friend, Charlie Henry—the three of us in the car together—and I couldn't help but think back to the days when my dad drove me to every practice and every game.

I'm not a storyteller, but I wanted to say a few words here about my life in hockey—not so much the details, which John Davidson writes about, but how it felt to be there.

I guess everybody has heard about the backyard rink at our family home in Brantford, Ontario. When I was two or three years old, my father would help me maneuver around the ice. By the time I was four or five, he'd started helping me improve my skating by teaching me turning and crossovers. He used to make the rink as big as he could, and since I was pretty small until I was about ten, there was always a lot of room out there. And the funny thing is that there were never a lot of other kids around. I don't remember picking up the phone and calling a lot of guys to come over and play games. I got more enjoyment out of shooting pucks and stickhandling by myself. I was really out there alone about 95 percent of the time.

My dad was a good teacher, a true fundamentalist who believed that anyone could be taught the basics of the game—skating and passing and stickhandling. There's a story that when we visited a hockey school in Russia in 1983, the coaches weren't interested in talking to Dad about drills and technique. That's not true. What is true is that a lot of the drills they were teaching their kids were the same as the ones he had taught me when I was growing up. (By the way, one of the kids at the camp the day we visited was Pavel Bure. He was only eleven or twelve years old then, but already everyone was saying watch out for this guy, he's pretty good!)

My dad was my first coach, but knew when to step back. The year I turned eleven, during the 1971-72 season, I scored 378 goals. Dad had coached my team for the previous three years, but he said, "I better not coach this year because people will get upset with the ice time you're going to have." It was my fifth season with the same team, and I was much better at the game than the other kids my age, so naturally I got more ice time and people treated me like a junior star. More and more, this became a problem for me in Brantford, and by the time I was fourteen my family and I felt that I should play in a stronger league. For this to happen, I had to move to Toronto and live with a family who became my legal guardians. I was going into Grade 9 and it was nice to be just one of the kids in school again. The same thing happened when I arrived in Sault Ste. Marie, Ontario to play Junior A in 1977: I boarded with another family. And when I moved to Edmonton in 1978, I stayed with relatives of the family who had billeted me in the Sault. Though I was now a professional player, I was still only seventeen years old.

I also stayed with my coach, Glen Sather, for two months in Edmonton. Glen got closer to his players than any NHL coach who had gone before him. If he thought he was having a problem with a player he would call him up and say, "Let's go get a bite to eat." There was always open communication there. Yes, he could be hard on us, and there were times when we got mad at him, but at the end of the day every player knew that Glen was a friend and that if you got into trouble he was the first guy you could call.

Gordie Howe, Gretzky, Mark Howe at the 1979 WHA All-Star game.

The Oilers were a team with a special spirit that started with Glen who passed it on to our captain, Lee Fogolin, and then on to guys like Kevin Lowe, Mark Messier and Glenn Anderson. What was amazing about this group was that our goal was always to win a championship, but we also pushed guys to be tremendous individual performers as well. We wanted Paul Coffey to win the Norris Trophy, and we wanted Messier to get 50 goals. We wanted Grant Fuhr to get a shutout. We always pushed for that. We wanted guys to be proud of what they accomplished. It wasn't that we wanted guys to be selfish, but we did want them to push themselves to the next level. And that all started with Glen. He brought that attitude from the Montreal Canadiens and the Boston Bruins. He'd played for both teams, and he'd learned that by both stressing teamwork and letting individual talents stand out—guys like Bobby Orr and Phil Esposito with the Bruins, and Guy Lafleur, Serge Savard and Ken Dryden with the Habs—you could win championships. That's what he brought to our team, and that's what we thrived on. People called us cocky, but in truth we were really just young and naïve. And we were good. Now that I'm retired I can say it: I was good.

When people remember those Oilers teams, they remember the offense and all the records we set, but it wasn't until we dedicated ourselves to working hard at playing an all-round game—concentrating on both offense and defense like the great Islanders teams of the early 1980s—that we became Stanley Cup champions.

Gretzky broke the NHL's single-season scoring record with 164 points in 1980-81. One season later, he would shatter this mark with 92 goals and 120 assists for 212 points.

Two of the best two-way players that I saw in my career were Oiler teammates. The first was Jari Kurri. People think of him as a goal scorer, but he was so good defensively that it allowed me to cheat on my defensive responsibilities. The second was Esa Tikkanen, my former left winger who, after I left the Oilers, was often assigned the task of shadowing me.

Of all the players who shadowed me over the years, Steve Kasper stands out. He was tough to play against because he cut off my angles, was smart and always played hard against me. It also didn't hurt him that he was often on the ice with Ray Bourque, a genuine superstar.

To me, though, just being able to shadow someone doesn't make you an all-round player, because it eliminates any offensive possibilities you might have. Another great two-way player was Guy Carbonneau. Over all the years I had to face him, he was always a threat offensively and defensively. He's a very intelligent player and he made my job difficult.

The most talented player I ever came up against was Mario Lemieux. When he came into the NHL, I wanted to show him that even though I was older and had played five seasons in the league, I still wanted to work hard and do well. I guess it was the same for me with Guy Lafleur and Marcel Dionne when I broke into the league. Everyone around us tried to build us up as rivals, but we never thought of ourselves that way.

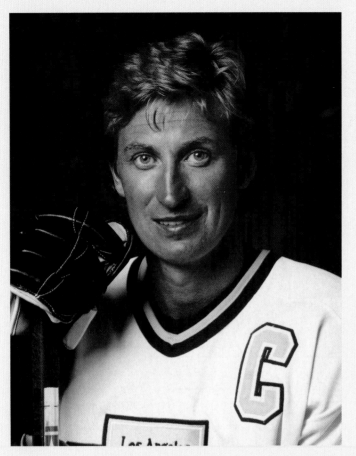

People have said that Mario learned from me at the Canada Cup in 1987, but there were a lot of Oilers on that team and we had all won the Stanley Cup three times. I think Mario watched all of us and used that experience to make himself a more complete player.

We won one more Stanley Cup together in Edmonton, but I knew during the 1988 finals that the Oilers were going to trade me: too many friends were telling me that Peter Pocklington had been calling around trying to sell me. Everybody had told my dad this too and he confirmed it with me before the final game. That's how I knew for sure. I didn't want to believe it, but deep down I knew the time had come. And a few weeks later, the deal was done.

As a member of the Los Angeles Kings, I quickly came to realize that being a Canadian hockey player living in the United States requires you to maintain a balance. You have to make people happy on both sides of the border. Sometimes it proved to be impossible, but I tried to wear both pairs of shoes. For example, the blue streak that followed the puck on Fox TV hockey broadcasts: from the point of view of a true fan of the game of hockey—from a Canadian's point of view—it didn't work. But from the point of view of the good of the game and trying to sell it to people who didn't know hockey, it was a great idea. And that's why I always try to see both points of view.

At the same time, Canadians are very proud of their country. I know I am. If a Canadian is racing against an American at the Olympics, I'll tell my wife and kids that the Canadian is going to win. As Canadians, we know we're a smaller country so we want to protect what we have. One thing we have is the game of hockey. That's ours. And I always try to remember that.

Still, when I got to Los Angeles, we had to promote hockey in the United States. I told Bruce McNall that we had to start at the grassroots. We needed to get kids wanting to play hockey and be hockey players. When that happened, they were going to tell their parents they wanted to go to NHL games. Of course, it didn't hurt that Mario was at the top of his game during that time, and Mark Messier was making the Rangers a success. Plus, Brett Hull was selling the game in the Midwest.

When I was traded to St. Louis in 1996, I really thought that I was going to finish my career there. My agent Michael Barnett and I negotiated with the Blues for three or four months to try to sign a long-term contract. As it turned out, that wasn't something they wanted. I think that upper management there questioned my ability and how much longer I was going to play. In my estimation, they really never stepped forward with any kind of a serious contract offer at all. So I signed with the Rangers.

I really enjoyed my time in New York City. What a great place to play! Such high energy inside the arena. It's the same buzz that you feel just walking around the city. And any player who's ever gone through it can tell you that—if you can win in New York, the people there will treat you like gold for the rest of your life. That's why the Rangers' playoff run when we reached the Conference finals in 1997 was one of the highlights of my career. I just wish we could have gone a little further.

The people of New York were always good to me. The way they cheered for me after my final game was amazing. But through the whole thing, I never wavered. There was never one time when I thought I might be making the wrong decision. All along, I kept on saying, "This is wonderful, but I'm happy it's coming to an end."

And it has. My career in the National Hockey League has given me a wonderful life, full of family, good friends and memories.

I hope you enjoy *99: My Life In Pictures*.

Wayne Gretzky
Thousand Oaks,
California
August 1999

Walter, Wayne and Glenn Gretzky, 1984.

The Meaning of Wayne

JOHN DAVIDSON

FOR A GUY WHO ALWAYS SEEMED TO BE AT THE TOP of every hockey list imaginable, Wayne Gretzky did not begin his NHL career at the top of the popularity chart.

It seems extremely odd to say that now. Because of what he has meant for hockey and the way he conducts himself, his popularity may be even greater today than at the height of his playing career. We've become good friends and I've been fortunate to have the opportunity to observe him in some truly remarkable episodes—both on and off the ice—demonstrating how unique, how exceptional he is as a player and an individual.

But at first, a lot of NHLers—myself included—didn't have such a high opinion of him. For years, we had all heard about him, and we marveled when we first saw him—this thin kid who wasn't very fast or powerful. We wondered why he was so good. But unless you were an Oiler fan, he was hard to like. Why? Because he was part of a young, cocky, brash—at times obnoxious—but extremely talented hockey club. Truthfully, some of the dislike was probably jealousy. They were so young and so good and over time we would grow to really enjoy them—the best offensive team ever assembled.

Glen Sather was the Oiler coach, and "Slats" was a brash, confident guy himself. But I wasn't surprised. He had been my teammate during my rookie season with the St. Louis Blues. I had been drafted in 1973 out of junior and jumped right into the NHL, the first junior goalie ever to make the jump. I was eighteen years old, pretty scared, and Glen and his wife were wonderful to me that year. In fact, when I got married, they gave us two Tennessee Walker horses as presents. It was good to see him back in the NHL when four former World Hockey Association clubs—the Oilers, Whalers, Nordiques and Jets—joined the league as part of an expansion in 1979-80.

I remember very clearly the first time they came into Madison Square Garden to face the Rangers in Gretzky's (and the Oilers') first NHL season. I think we won the game.

But they could have had three or four goals—they just didn't finish. Very clearly, I recall a play near the net. There was a pass from behind which came out front, from my right to my left. I think Gretzky made the pass, and it was a hell of a good one. The puck came across and found his winger, who must have been Blair McDonald, but he just missed the open net. This was in the second period, so the Oilers bench was closest to me. I can still hear Slats, my old friend, from the bench, yelling at me, "Davidson you lucky son of a bitch!" With their attitude, you'd have thought bad luck was the only reason they didn't win. We had gone to the Stanley Cup finals the previous spring and we were a pretty good team. They were a bunch of kids, but the way these guys carried on, you'd have thought that it had been the Oilers who had beaten us to win the Stanley Cup instead of the Montreal Canadiens. Still, you had to admit this was not an ordinary team. They were fast and there was something energetic, something special about these guys.

And Gretz, of course, was their centerpiece. That whole period of his career, when he was young—still a teenager—he drove everyone nuts. He was thin. He was spindly. He was also really good. And he played with a lot of raw emotion. When he got mad at one of the opposition players or at a referee, he didn't hesitate to express himself. They used to call him "The Whiner." On the bench or in the dressing room, guys would say, "What a piece of work he is!" In hockey, the unwritten rule is that you face adversity like a man. When a young player is really talkative like that on the ice, someone on the other team will usually try to, shall we say, straighten him out. Guys on the Rangers would tell him to shut his yap. I'm sure this happened everywhere.

But the funny thing is, it never really went beyond that. One reason was that Dave Semenko was always around and he would skate by you to say hello. And if you tried anything, he'd knock your head off.

Still, with Gretzky's size and his attitude, the thinking was, "How is this guy going to last?"

I only played against Wayne a few times. I remember going up to Edmonton early in his NHL career. Gretzky got hurt that game, and they carried him off the ice. But he came back and set up the game winner. That should have been a clue right there. No one ever had more determination. It is one of the themes of his career, which saw him lead four Stanley Cup teams in five years, win international championships for Canada, become the NHL all-time leading scorer and set or share 61 records listed in the *NHL Guide and Record Book* (40 in regular-season play, 15 in Stanley Cup play and six in All-Star Games). But at virtually every step of his triumphant journey, a chorus of doubters questioned everything—his achievements, his skating, his size, his sweater number (which made his back the most photographed in sports), his ever-changing hairstyles and, yes, his youthful on-ice demeanor—eager to expose some limit on talent that seemed unlimited. With the passage of time, the mountain of trophies and his exceptional grace under pressure, it's easy to forget how skeptical people were, just as we've forgotten that Bobby Orr was charged with not minding his end of the ice and Gordie Howe was once considered a big, lazy hockey player.

In Gretzky's case, his critics' blind spot was that they thought emotional runts weren't supposed to be the best players on the ice; rock-hard, scar-faced warriors were.

In hindsight, the doubters probably spurred him on. As his first biographer, Jim Taylor, wrote in the *Calgary Sun*, "He wanted to play minor hockey at age five at a time when it didn't start until age 10. They wouldn't let him. He went home and practiced and showed up again when he was six. If they'd said no again, he'd have gone home, practiced some more, and turned up when he was seven. Maybe they knew that, because this time they said yes to a scared under-age pip-squeak lost in a forest of 10-year-olds. Besides, coach Dick Martin had noticed something. 'As soon as he got the puck,' he said, 'he wasn't frightened anymore.' It was a thread that ran through all the childhood stories: If you told him it couldn't be done, doing it became a crusade."

Gretzky scored only one goal that first season for the Nadrofsky Steelers in Brantford, Ontario, in his team's final game—"It's the only time I ever felt overmatched," he once said—but Martin recognized he was a better stickhandler than the 10-year-olds and an excellent skater. For that, for just about everything, credit his parents.

A humble man and woman (who would not walk away from a phone company job or a home on Varadi Avenue for the life on Easy Street their grown-up eldest son would one day offer), Walter and Phyllis Gretzky devoted their abundant energies to their family. The backyard at 42 Varadi

Wayne notched his first 100-goal season at age nine.

became a community skating rink, "Wally's Coliseum," where Walter's sons learned the fundamentals of hockey and his daughter Kim practiced figure skating, where the neighborhood kids scrimmaged three on three, where Wayne prodded next-door neighbor Brian Rizzetto to play goal long after sundown so he could practice his backhand. "Sometimes," Walter told Taylor. "you had to argue to get him to come in at night."

If some master plan authorized Wally's Coliseum, it wasn't Wally's. "I didn't flood the backyard to build a hockey star," he said. "I flooded it so I could watch from the kitchen, where it was warm."

He did more than watch, he taught, down to the detail of making cones for skating drills out of plastic jugs. Walter's drills must have been far ahead of their time; Gretzky once spoke of the novel practice techniques used by the 1972 Soviet National Team which amazed the North American hockey establishment during the Summit Series: "I'd been doing those drills since I was three. My dad was very smart." He still teaches today. Whenever we talk about his Dad, Wayne inevitably brings up Walter's continuing dedication to hockey. On a Rangers' charter flight around Christmas of 1998, Wayne told me, with this amazed tone in his voice, that Walter wasn't home for the holiday: "Do you know he's still coaching kids? Do you know he's over in Sweden right now with a kids' team?" As award-winning author Roy MacGregor wrote, without exaggeration, in his best-selling book, *The Home Team: Fathers, Sons & Hockey*, Walter would become "the most famous father in his country."

After the end-of-season banquet following that first year, Wayne cried during the car ride home.

"What's wrong?" his father asked.

"I didn't win a trophy. Everyone won a trophy but me."

"Wayne, keep practicing and one day you're gonna have so many trophies, we're not going to have room for them all."

Wally's lessons began paying off. In Wayne's second season, he scored 27 goals. The next year, 1969-70, he scored 104 and added 63 assists in 62 games. Nearly 10 years old as the following season began, finally the same age as the rest of the league, he scored 196 goals and 120 assists in 76 games. Then, in the 82 games of the 1971-72 campaign, he totaled an astonishing 378 goals and 139 assists.

The national spotlight found him that year, when Canadian Press called Gretzky "a four-foot-four, 78-pound dynamo." He was filling local arenas. He confessed to becoming somewhat shy around older teammates, but they still got along quite well. However, some envious parents openly expressed their displeasure with his style of play. At first, skeptical adults considered Wayne's performances at best flukes; later, catcalls rained down on him. He was accused, though not by teammates, of hogging the puck, depriving other players of attention and scoring opportunities. Envious stopwatches clocked his ice time.

Among the values imparted by Walter and Phyllis, proper respect was paramount, toward adults and other kids. It's a lesson Wayne has taken to heart as much as any he learned on the backyard rink. "You're no better or no worse than anyone," the Gretzkys told their children. "Everyone is equal. Some are just more fortunate than others."

As the media circled Varadi Avenue, Walter dispensed a little extra advice. "You're a very special person," he told Wayne. "Wherever you go, probably all your life, people are going to make a fuss over you. You've got to remember that and you've got to behave right. They're going to be watching for every mistake. Remember that. You're very special and you're on display."

Brantford's small-town jealousies occasionally upset Wayne and especially angered Phyllis. "I think that part of my life shaped my personality," he wrote in his 1990 autobiography. "For one thing, I grew up fast. I had the world's shortest childhood. By the time I was 13, I had an agent....I had seen adults at their best and their worst. I learned that jealousy is the worst disease in life. And I learned that there are always going to be some people who want to bronze you and some who want to hang you and you can't get too carried away with either kind. Because I was afraid to be thought of as cocky or mouthy, I became even more shy. Enough people disliked me just for the way I played hockey, I didn't want to start talking and give them something else not to like. I didn't want to get anyone hurt."

It's somewhat miraculous the atmosphere didn't kill his passion for the game, the characteristic which allowed his talents to develop. But the passion had been there from the start. If Walter's biggest lesson to Wayne had been "Go where the puck's going, not where it's been," young Wayne had happily reinforced it by sitting in front of the TV with a pad and pencil watching Hockey Night In Canada. He'd draw a rink diagram on the pad and when the puck was dropped, he'd watch the screen and trace the movements of the puck on the diagram. He did this over and over, and

The 18-year-old pro. Taping up before his final game in the World Hockey Asociation, 1979.

then he'd study the diagrams. That helped him learn the areas of the rink where the puck was likely to go.

The Gretzkys finally coped with Brantford by reluctantly allowing Wayne to enter a Junior B program in Toronto, a 14-year-old playing against 20-year-olds. On the ice, he continued to excel, clearing the hurdles of his lesser age, size and strength. But separated from his family, it was a lonely existence. "I didn't leave Brantford to play better hockey," he said. "I left because people drove me out." He would never live at home again.

Moving to Junior A hockey with the Soo Greyhounds at 16, an age when most players are overjoyed just to feel their way through the pro-style environment, Gretzky made a training camp pledge to his coach Muzz McPherson: He'd break the league scoring record. And he did, too, although he pushed Ottawa's star Bobby Smith to stay a step ahead of him and Smith set the new record. Their rivalry was headline news in Ontario and fueled their competitive fires. One night in Ottawa, McPherson rested Gretzky in the third period with his team trailing 4–1. Gretzky was insulted, interpreting the move as a benching. Sent out on the power play with seven minutes remaining, the angered 16-year-old asked McPherson sarcastically, "You want me to win it or tie it?"

"A tie would be lovely," the coach responded.

Gretzky scored three goals. A teammate told McPherson, "You made a mistake, Coach. You should have told him to win it."

Word got out that Gretzky would turn pro at 17 and that's when most of us in the NHL started to notice him. We knew there was this young kid in Eastern Canada who was a great scorer but, despite the gaudy numbers, no one dreamed he was that good. He was too young to play in the NHL, but the WHA set no age restrictions. His eye-opening jump into the pro ranks got tons of publicity. Howie Meeker, once the NHL Rookie of the Year and an outspoken TV commentator, said, "I know he can out-think and outsmart the others and his skating is not that bad. But turn pro at 17? He'd get killed" playing against men in the WHA.

But Gretzky took it as another challenge and, playing briefly for Indianapolis, then for Edmonton, he finished third in scoring, with 110 points, trailing only two veterans—Quebec's Buddy Cloutier, who had 129 points, and Cincinnati's Robbie Ftorek with 116. He captured rookie of the year honors, a second all-star team selection and, in the WHA All-Stars three-game series against Moscow Dynamo, scored two goals (including the series opener) while playing on a line with his hockey hero, 50-year-old Gordie Howe, and Gordie's son, Mark.

When the WHA died and the Oilers moved to the NHL, they already had assembled some pieces of their great nucleus, and within three seasons, they were all there—Gretzky, Mark Messier, Kevin Lowe, Jari Kurri, Paul Coffey, Glenn Anderson, Grant Fuhr and Andy Moog.

As brash as Slats was, he also has more street smarts than anyone I know. You can't underestimate the job he did leading those kids, including Gretzky. On the ice he recognized he had a young team with a tremendous amount of talent and he never suppressed it. He turned it loose. And in the dressing room, he built unity among them by fostering an "Us Against The World" attitude. And it worked. That's why they acted so cocky.

As it turned out, the Oilers weren't bad guys at all. Early in my broadcasting career, I worked out of Western Canada and covered the Oilers when they were in the process of becoming champions. They were amazingly talented, but as an ex-player myself, I got great enjoyment out of watching them grow together. Everyone suspected that their high-powered hockey machine had big-time attitude, but once you got around their dressing room or the bench at the morning skate on a game day, there was no arrogance. From Slats to players like Kevin Lowe, Charlie Huddy and Lee Fogolin, talking to them was like talking to someone you might meet at a restaurant or local bar. You might find yourself talking to Charlie Huddy, leaning against the boards after practice, schmoozing about anything and everything. It was a telltale sign that this team could play a very relaxed game. For the most part, they had fun, while some other teams always struggled dealing with the burden of self-imposed pressure and expectations. But these guys knew how to enjoy the moment, how to have fun on and off the ice.

Like the entire Oilers team, I think Wayne was a bit misunderstood. Although he did some yapping and whining and had fist-pumping, arm-windmilling goal celebrations, he really didn't intend to show anybody up, although that may have been how it was perceived. He wasn't a trash talker. He had—and still has—an enormous respect for the game. But sometimes you've got to find a way from within to get your talents out, to be the best you can. Wayne always responded to challenges, that was

one way, and another way was these verbal outbursts and his celebrations. I think he used them to motivate himself.

Over the years, those characteristics largely disappeared as Wayne's confidence grew and he became more mature. His skill level was always very high, but he became tough—really tough, mentally tough.

Mental toughness is two things. First, it's the ability to play well in the big games, getting yourself prepared to outthink an opponent on the ice. Second, it's mental endurance. Think about the amount of hockey a top player plays per game, the amount he plays per season, the number of big games he plays, including playoffs. And on top of all that are the demands off the ice, which fall under the endurance category. The guy's at the gas station filling up his car and he signs autographs. He's at the airport waiting for his luggage, he gets off the team bus at the hotel, people are waiting for him. You can play a game in Dallas, get on the plane, land in Tampa Bay at 4 a.m., at 4:45 you get to the hotel and there's a line of people waiting for autographs. Even the average star needs great endurance to put up with that celebrity and still perform on the ice, but with Wayne, the demand seems infinitely larger and never-ending. Traveling with him, you see people constantly tugging at him, but he knows how to handle it. He has somehow mastered his energy. Today you see a man who always has time for people—teammates, media or family. To become that person, having been this kid, this spindly, emotional little guy, I find that an amazing transformation.

One thing that never changed was his incredible hunger to get the job done. Another thing that hovered around him for years were the skeptics, who most certainly didn't disappear once he reached the NHL. "He's too small," they said. "He's certainly not strong, and his frame won't stand

Gretzky averaged more that 203 points per season from 1982 to 1987, bringing #99 special attention whenever he played.

up to the pounding night after night."

Gretzky responded the way he knew best, by playing great hockey.

About two months into his first season, he was playing pretty well when the Oilers pulled into Toronto and he picked up a local newspaper. In it, a sports columnist complimented Gretzky on adjusting to the NHL, but warned readers not to confuse the NHL with the WHA, that a third place finish in scoring in this league would be too much for anyone to expect.

An incensed Gretzky resolved to prove the writer wrong. Figuring only Guy Lafleur and Marcel Dionne would outpoint him, he aimed for that third spot and turned up his game. April came and found Lafleur finishing third. Young Wayne totaled 51 goals and a league best 86 assists. Dionne ended up with two more goals and two fewer assists. The NHL awarded Dionne the Art Ross Trophy as leading scorer on the basis of most goals scored. But the 19-year-old Gretzky was voted the Hart Trophy as NHL MVP.

Still, some people had trouble believing he was that good. "Let's see him do it again next season," they said. He answered them by rewriting the *NHL Official Guide & Record Book*.

The next season, he set new NHL standards for assists and points, with 109 and 164 respectively.

In 1981-82, he banged in the fastest 50 goals ever, in 39 games (including four in game 38 and five in game 39), shattering the 50-in-50 mold first cast by Rocket Richard in 1945 and equaled by Mike Bossy in 1981. He tied Phil Esposito's single season mark of 76 goals in his 63rd game and got a hat trick in his 64th. He finished with an incredible 92 goals and a stratospheric 212 points.

"The NHL has changed," the critics grumbled. "Rocket Richard, Jean Beliveau, Gordie Howe and Bobby Hull all took more punishment in one game than Gretzky takes in a season."

The proud Richard replied, "I have now seen Gretzky enough to say that in whatever decade he played, he would've been the scoring champion."

In 1982-83, he elevated his assist record to 125 and won his fourth consecutive Hart Trophy, surpassing Bobby Orr's feat of three straight set a decade earlier.

In 1983-84, he added a fifth Hart and fourth Ross to his collection. He scored in the first game of the season and just didn't stop collecting points, passing Lafleur's previous record streak in the 29th game. He wasn't kept off the score sheet until game 52. Losing six games to injury, he still scored 87 goals.

"No one plays defense anymore," the skeptics moaned. "The game is so wide open, no wonder he breaks records."

"Then why hasn't anyone else done what Wayne Gretzky's done?" asked Philadelphia's Bobby Clarke, whose own competitive spirit made him one of Gretzky's

role models. "I'll tell you why. Because he's that much better than the rest of us."

In 1984-85, Gretzky upped his assist mark to 135, and won his fifth consecutive Art Ross Trophy, a new record. His plus/minus rating of +98 became the highest figure ever recorded by a forward.

In 1985-86 more Hart and Ross awards, but this time Wayne broke through his own ceiling with 215 points and a dizzying 163 assists.

"He doesn't play defense. All he does is hang around the fringes looking to pick up points."

"He doesn't get credit for it," remarked Scotty Bowman, the NHL's all-time winningest coach, "but I think Gretzky's the best forechecker in the NHL today. A lot of great scorers had other guys who got the puck and got it to them. Gretzky gets a lot of pucks himself. He plays so well without the puck."

By this time he could no longer be labeled a "fluke," so Canadian screenwriter Jay Teitel pondered another possibility:

> He must have been doing it with mirrors. He had to be, we knew, because the more we watched him play the more we realized one basic truth: He was the least physically dominating—and so the most physically perplexing—star in modern sports. He was quick enough, but not terrifically fast, his shot was ordinary (he wound up ridiculously high on his slapshot), his style could best be described as herky-jerky, or maybe spikey (of all the great contemporary athletes, only Magic Johnson had a style as idiosyncratic or unlikely), and half the time he looked half-exhausted. Worse than exhausted, with his sweater hiked over the right side of his pants—a superstitious holdover from the day his father had tucked in six-year-old Wayne's sweater so it wouldn't impede his shot—he looked like the perpetual over-cool, cocky sloppy kid playing with the big boys, the kid everyone else had conspired to let succeed ('Let him have the puck; he's just a kid').

It all seemed incomprehensible. So how did he do it?

The days and nights in Wally's Coliseum laid the foundation, but upon that he had constructed the damnedest combination of techniques anyone had ever seen. His work habits in practice were exemplary, his thirst for knowledge about the game unquenchable. Colin Campbell, Gretzky's teammate when the Oilers joined the NHL, remembers that, as an 18-year-old, "he was older than his years in how he perceived the game and how he approached it. He had great intuition. He loved to talk about the game. He loved to learn. He soaked up every possible bit of information. He loved to go to watch other games, like if we'd go into a town early and the home team played another team, he'd go to that game. Most young guys who come up have other things on their minds when they get a night off."

He processed all that information into his thinking. Just

as those with photographic memories can read a paragraph once and recite it back to you, or hear a passage of music and immediately perform it themselves, Gretzky was blessed with a similar capacity for the game of hockey. Quite simply, he had a gift for recognizing the sport's patterns and that allowed him to execute more creatively, more quickly and more successfully than anyone else. It was like he had a computer chip in his head—and this was long before personal computers. He had a genius for the game. He was hockey's Einstein.

Scouts and coaches started talking about things like his "sense of anticipation," his "lateral mobility" and his ability to "see the whole ice," phrases that now have become part of the sport's vocabulary.

"When you grade the talents we normally look for in young players," said one scout, "it's almost spooky how he does it. The puck just comes to him."

"I let the puck do the work," Gretzky stated.

His thinking was far ahead of everyone else's. He became very innovative on faceoff plays. He and Jari Kurri developed a play where, when everyone was set for the drop of the puck, Kurri backed out away from the circle to an unoccupied area and Wayne would win the draw back to him; Kurri would take the puck and, with his great shot—bang!—one-time it off the pass. If Gretzky noticed the opposition had failed to position a player along the boards on a face-off, he'd whack the puck to that open spot and recover it to start the play. He was always thinking.

To be honest, it was not easy to play with him. Gretzky's hockey intellect posed difficulties for many—not Kurri, of course, with whom he shared an on-ice ESP. And in 1986, Esa Tikkanen joined them, solving the long-standing problem of getting a left wing who fit Gretzky's style. But in his post-Edmonton days, his teams often had trouble finding complementary players. Very few could perform at the same mental level. Mario Lemieux did in the '87 Canada Cup, as did Steve Larmer during their European barnstorming tour in '94. Niklas Sundstrom also had some good chemistry with Wayne in New York. But many who have tried couldn't match his quick thought process. Nor did they have a quick enough stick. Having a quick stick was crucial, because of how fast Gretz could put the puck right on his teammate's blade when it wasn't expected. Many players either panicked or just reacted too slowly.

Gretzky's trademark became his play behind the net. He started doing it when he played as a teenager in Toronto, looking for a spot on the ice where he wouldn't get knocked down by defenders. He says he got it from Bobby Clarke, who was good back there. Bernie Federko in St. Louis was also effective from that spot, but Wayne raised it to another level. Lou Nanne, who coached the Minnesota North Stars, once joked that the only way to defend against him was to push the net back against the endboards.

When Wayne set up behind the net, boy, that was really hard for goaltenders! I can tell you that from personal experience. First you start guessing, "Is he going backhand or forehand?" Nobody could saucer a puck more accurately. Even if Wayne was playing in tight quarters and had to make a four-foot pass, he could put it over two blades, hit his teammate's stick and, bang! it was in the net.

Another concern for the goaltender when Gretz was

Despite nine seasons with more than 50 goals, it is Gretzky's skills as a setup man that might prove to be matchless. He led the NHL in assists for 13 consecutive seasons beginning in 1979-80.

behind you was, "Which side is he going to come out on, right or left?" You've got to get your stick down to try and intercept the pass, even though he could put it over your stick.

And of course you've got to worry about the player in front waiting for the pass. "Where does he go? Does he stay on one side, does he move in front, does he move to the other side, does he back out? What does he do?"

I had a trick though. I would watch the eyes of the forward in front. He would be following Gretzky, so you could go wherever his eyes were going. That was one way to try stopping him.

But, as effective as that play could be, Wayne didn't stop there. He also taught himself how to use the metal frame of the net to pass the puck back to himself or to a teammate.

He spent hours in practice banking the puck off different parts of the frame from all sorts of angles to see where the puck would go.

Perfecting these plays, creating all these options out of a tight space behind the net, just illustrated Wayne's advanced understanding of the game. He took the net and made it a shield. He knew it would cause problems for the defending team—you're trying to do three or four things at once—so he would attempt to exploit a weakness. If you only counted the points he scored on plays from behind the net, it wouldn't surprise me if they alone would be enough to win all those scoring titles.

If setting up behind the net was revolutionary, so was Wayne's play once he crossed the blue line. Coaches had forever instructed their forwards to go to the net when they entered the zone, and defenders knew what to expect. But Wayne realized he could be more creative if he added a few twists once he reached the zone. The first was the curl, in which he'd cross the line and then curl toward the boards, holding the puck and waiting for a teammate to get open for a pass when he completed his curl. That was how the concept of the "late man" entering the play developed, because the defenders and backcheckers had picked up the first offensive players in the zone but someone could follow the play and be open for a pass. Herb Brooks had us doing things like that when he took the Rangers to Finland for training camp in 1982. It was a big departure from how we had been taught to play. Guys were saying, "What the hell is going on here?" and it required some big adjustments. But Herbie was right and our team—soon to be known to its fans as the "Smurfs"—confused a lot of clubs when we figured out how to do it.

Well, Gretz did that all the time and it became something else he raised to another level. Paul Coffey became the perfect late man because his incredible speed easily freed him from defensive coverage. Wayne would cross the blue line, curl, Coffey would come in late and—bam!—Gretz would hit him in the high slot with a pass and create a great scoring opportunity. It was one of the most effective of the Oilers' many offensive weapons.

As a variation, Gretz would cross the line and, rather than curl, cut across the zone laterally. The defenders would be caught backing in and he gained time and space to shoot or pass. He scored a lot of goals that way, cutting into the high slot, using one of those backing defensemen to create a screen and then slapping the puck.

"When I played against him," recalls Colin Campbell, "you just couldn't stop him. Maybe he didn't pass the puck like Perreault or shoot like Mike Bossy or have the brute strength of Mark Messier, but he did just about everything better than everyone else. You didn't know how to stop him. He just had a magical touch.

"One of the big questions of the 1980s was 'Why don't you hit him?' Well," Campbell chuckles, "you couldn't."

How did he survive, being a smaller man in what increasingly has become a big man's game? Some small players succeeded by playing dirty or nasty, but Gretz won the Lady Byng Trophy for gentlemanly play in his first year, his last year and three other times. He had an entirely different approach to the game's physical dimension.

Wayne figured out that by combining skating and body positioning, he could play in traffic and not suffer the consequences. It's hardly unusual for athletes to use their bodies to supplement the activity of their arms. Boxers, golfers, tennis players, baseball players, hockey players all increase the effectiveness of their skill by moving their bodies to increase the power of their arm movements. But Gretzky did something unique. He could get the pass off, put it right on a player's stick and maneuver himself to fall off the check. It was like a fadeaway jump shot. And it was remarkable to watch guys try to hit him and then go flying into the boards or the glass, while he would just shift away and be off down the ice.

Where did that come from? "Wayne was a heck of a lacrosse player until the other sports got in the way and he had to drop the game," said Walter. "He had a great touch with the stick. He could shoot, he could pass, he could roll off a check—a skill he took with him into hockey."

Checkers noticed it, too. "It's no good trying to line him up for a hard check; he's too mobile," said Boston's Steve Kasper, one of the most effective "shadows" Gretzky encountered. "If you start lunging at him, he'll make you look ridiculous."

"He's never really committed in one direction," observed Hall of Fame goaltender Ken Dryden. "His body is always moving in a number of ways. In Bobby Orr, you sensed more power, more commitment. Gretzky will just sort of collapse in the direction you hit him."

Although usually near or at the bottom in strength tests, he was much stronger than he looked, and he used that strength in surprising ways. When he checked, he often came from behind, chasing the opposition from somewhere deep in the other team's zone; he was always deep so if the opposing defenseman or forward came up with the puck, they'd head up ice rather than having to clear the zone. But Gretz would catch the puck carrier and frequently lift the guy's stick from behind or tug at him—not enough to take a penalty—but enough to strip the guy of the puck. That takes strength at the NHL level. He was quicker and stronger than people believed—and a lot better defensively. Perhaps he didn't always backcheck, but he and the Oilers were so dangerous with the puck, and had it so often, it was your team that was forced into a defensive posture, not his.

Wayne was setting records and so were the Oilers. They poured a gusher of goals into enemy nets as no team had before, becoming the first team—and they remain the only team—ever to score 400 goals in a season, a feat they accomplished in five consecutive years, starting in 1981-82. But their scoring prowess did not guarantee the big silver mug and neither Gretzky nor his teammates would consider their careers a success until the Stanley Cup had been won. The Stanley Cup playoffs require the highest level of play in hockey, each round more grueling than the last. It is acknowledged by athletes from all sports that the Cup is the hardest championship to win among the team sports. And in the court of public opinion, winning the Cup is often the dividing line between being a good player and being a great player. In Wayne's case, not winning the Cup was the unscratchable itch that kept the critics howling.

In the Oilers' second trip to the playoffs, they swept the mighty 1981 Canadiens. That series was probably best known for the remarks made by Montreal goalie Richard Sevigny, who predicted Lafleur would put Gretzky "in his back pocket." The Flower finished with one point in three games; Gretzky had a goal and five assists in game one and hat tricks in games two and three. When Gretzky was on the ice with the teams at even strength, the Oilers outscored the Habs 11-0. The defending champion Islanders knocked out Edmonton in the next round, but they needed six games in which to do it in a well contested series. Again the young Oilers drew attention, this time by singing "Here we go Oilers, here we go" on the bench, acting, in the words of one writer, "like a bunch of high school kids."

"Sure, it was high schoolish, but we were all barely out of high school." Gretzky later said. "We didn't know yet how to be cool, unflappable, unemotional professionals."

They received a big dose of professional hockey reality in the next spring's opening round. The Kings finished 47 points behind the Smythe Division champion Oilers, who scored 417 goals and improved 37 points over the previous season, but Edmonton's inexperience was revealed. In the first game, the Oilers blew a 4–1 lead and fell 10-8. Then, in the legendary "Miracle on Manchester" game three, the Oilers led 5-0 in the third but surrendered the tying goal in the last minute of the third period and then lost in overtime. A gutsy win facing elimination in game four was not repeated in the deciding game five in Edmonton, where a second-period collapse led to a 7–4 defeat.

The Oilers still had lessons to learn in 1982-83. Deflated but not defeated, they soothed themselves by scoring 424 goals in the regular season. That spring, without singing, they advanced to the finals before being swept by the defensively excellent Islanders. Gretzky began authoring new playoff records, with 26 assists and 38 points over the four rounds of the playoffs, but he went without a goal in the finals, to the critics' delight.

But something happened as Gretzky and Kevin Lowe made their way to the bus parked under the Islanders' Nassau Coliseum. They had to walk by the Isles' dressing room, which they dreaded since they knew the enemy would be wildly celebrating, but as they did, they noticed that the team staff and the players' families were whooping it up, while the Islanders themselves were icing injuries, getting rubdowns, limping and sporting black eyes. "It looked more like a morgue in there than a champion's locker room," Gretzky recalled. "And here we were looking perfectly fine and healthy."

Then Lowe said something Gretzky would never forget: "That's how you win championships."

It was time to grow, and perhaps that was what Lee Fogolin had in mind when he voluntarily relinquished his Oiler captaincy and Sather had Lyle "Sparky" Kulchisky, the Oilers' assistant trainer, sew the captain's "C" on sweater number 99 during the fall '83 training camp. As we came to know, Messier and Lowe were also very strong leaders for that Oiler team, but Wayne was an extremely effective captain. Much of his leadership came on the ice. He occasionally spoke up in the room as well and all indications are that it was always on target. When he spoke, he certainly had his teammates' attention because it came from the heart. But most of what made him a good captain was what he did on the ice, where all good captains must lead. Steve Yzerman is much like Gretzky in that respect—he does it on the ice and he saves his talking for certain times. If you're too rah-rah, if you overextend yourself too many times, your teammates can tune out. They may listen, but they won't digest it. With Wayne, the quality of his leadership was more in the way he carried himself on and off the ice and how he treated people.

Gretzky accepted the responsibility of leading the Oilers to the top and they wound up the 1983-84 season first overall with 119 points, at the time the sixth-best total ever. Haunted by the ghosts of playoffs past, they concentrated on team defense and cut a full goal a game off their regular season average, returning to the finals for a rematch with the Islanders.

New York had eliminated the Oilers twice before, had defeated Edmonton in 10 straight regular-season games and had just captured their 19th consecutive playoff series, but they were a battered, banged-up crew. The Oilers were younger, healthier and faster. And they were not afraid to pay the price this time, hitting the Islanders at every opportunity. They had world-class forwards, centered by Gretzky and Messier, who played a high-tempo game, but they also had third and fourth liners—Kevin McClelland, Dave Lumley, Pat Conacher, Dave Semenko, Dave Hunter, Ken Linseman—who could really muck, grind and hit. Their defenders—Lowe, Huddy, Randy Gregg, Pat Hughes—could also play it tough.

So on the evening of May 19, 1984, with the home team leading 5–2 late in the third period of game five, Oiler fan Sandy Monteith mounted a staircase in the stands of the Northlands Coliseum, wearing a construction hard hat upon which he had mounted a miniature Stanley Cup. He ignited a mixture of flashpowder and gunpowder, shooting

Playing for keeps: Combative Islanders goaltender Billy Smith stands his ground during the 1983 Stanley Cup finals won by New York in a four-game sweep.

body and so on. The tactic succeeded in Chicago's first two home games, where they had the last change, and that evened the series at two games apiece. But the overpowering Oilers still averaged over seven goals per game to win the six-game series. They then made quick work of the upstart Philadelphia Flyers in the 1985 finals, and Gretzky's new playoff standards of 30 assists and 47 points earned him the Conn Smythe Trophy as Stanley Cup MVP.

But with talk of a dynasty thick in the air, the Oilers came crashing down to earth a year later. In a seventh game against a physical Calgary team, young Oiler defenseman Steve Smith accidentally banked the puck off Fuhr's heel into his own net, giving the Flames a shocking second round win.

How could this happen to hockey's most talented squad? It was the hottest topic on hockey's summer grapevine. I can say with great certainty, there was no rivalry like Edmonton–Calgary in the 1980s. The rivalries between the Rangers–Islanders, Montreal–Quebec and Montreal–Boston were tremendous, but none of them matched the Battle of Alberta, so-named because the Oilers–Flames encounters were absolute wars, with these guys knocking the stuffing out of each other. Both teams had talent, passion, leadership, great general managers and great coaches. Bob Johnson in Calgary deserves great credit for his innovations as the Flames coach, for he actually came up with the left-wing lock that the Detroit Red Wings have used to such great advantage in the 1990s. For Johnson, the tactic was a necessity since the Oilers right side was extremely dangerous. With Gretzky feeding Kurri and Messier feeding Anderson, Johnson was forced to keep his left side back.

Though fingers were pointed and speculation posed as explanation, the truth was that the Oilers did not follow their coaches' game plan, abandoning their forechecking, and falling victim to overconfidence. It was left to captain Gretzky to issue a new challenge to his teammates: "If we expect to win another Cup, we'll have to take a lot more punishment, both physically and mentally."

A mature, more businesslike demeanor arose at Northlands. It may be only coincidental that, apart from winning the Hart and Ross, the 1986-87 season was the first in which Gretzky did not set some sort of individual scor-

a three-foot high flame up and out of the little Cup's bowl, lighting the baptismal fire of a new champion.

And a new King of the Ice was anointed—the Oilers' captain, number 99, again the top post-season scorer. He hoisted the large silver chalice of dreams overhead and gazed at his reflection on its surface. The Islanders—and the critics—were defeated.

Edmonton's blend of North American strength and European speed and skill now made them hockey's biggest attraction. Undefeated in their first 15 games the next season (still a record) they played like interlocking parts of a fluid machine, moving the puck with pinball dynamics. With two fine goaltenders in Fuhr and Moog, they would just turn up the jets and go.

In the Conference Championships in the spring of 1985, the Oilers faced Chicago. The Blackhawks had hired Roger Neilson as a special assistant coach and he developed a game plan to throw Edmonton off balance in which each line had a different role when they went on the ice. Depending on which Oilers line went over the boards, Chicago would try matching with a line to exploit a supposed Edmonton weakness; the Denis Savard line would push forward, another line would trap, one line took the ing record. One wonders if greater leadership burdens came at the expense of his personal statistics. If so, he made the trade gladly. A seven-game victory over the Flyers returned the Cup to his hands in May 1987. And from his hands, Gretzky—again the playoffs' leading scorer—passed Lord Stanley's trophy directly to Steve Smith, ending the defenseman's year-long nightmare.

It was always fascinating to watch the Oilers' reactions when they won the Cup. The way they handed the trophy off from one to another was genuine. In fact, it may be that they were the first NHL team to do that—to allow each player a chance to skate with the Cup right after winning. They made certain the McClellands, Hunters and Semenkos felt every bit as important in victory as the Kurris and Andersons. They certainly established a few traditions, such as when Wayne gathered the entire team around him to have their photo taken with the Cup on the ice. Fans remember these kinds of special moments and they lead to more creative celebrations, such as when Scotty Bowman laced 'em up and skated with his players after winning the Cup in Detroit.

But Gretzky's passing of the Cup to Steve Smith truly indicated the caliber of person he is. Any number of captains might have gotten lost in the moment of winning the championship and just celebrated; no one would have faulted a captain who had not thought such a gesture was necessary. To Wayne, it was necessary.

Teammates, close friends and Stanley Cup champions in Edmonton: Gretzky and Mark Messier.

A glorious Canada Cup triumph over the Soviets climaxed by Gretzky's marvelous pass to Mario Lemieux for the series winner, closed with hockey's two super-novas hugging in triumph. For a moment, the voices of dissent were settled. All was right with the world, but beneath the surface, forces churned. Players wanted more money, ownership resisted. It is a daily story today, but in the NHL of 1987, it was unsettling. The Oilers began to disintegrate.

Trading Paul Coffey, who had held out, meant the defense generated less offense, and Edmonton's goals sank to 365, their lowest since 1981. Gretzky missed 16 games due to injury and for the first time won neither the Hart nor the Ross. The Oilers' second-place finish ended six seasons at the top. Lemieux captured much of the hardware that spring and the big barrel seemed up for grabs.

The 1988 playoffs were the weirdest ever, fully equipped with an officials' walkout and a power blackout. Gretzky even sported a severe crewcut. But the Oilers knocked off Winnipeg (Gretzky setting up 10 goals in five games), then Calgary (his game two overtime winner the pivotal moment). The Oilers then took on Detroit.

Here's a small example of Wayne's singular approach to hockey, and also an illustration of just how accommodating he was with the media. In 1987, I was working for Global TV covering the Oilers-Red Wings Conference Championship. As a broadcaster in this situation, I desperately wanted to talk to Gretzky, but I also knew it was a big series, and he might be too focused to give me what I needed.

It was a couple of hours before the game, and outside the Oilers' dressing room Wayne was working on his sticks. Despite my fears, he started the conversation: "Hey John, how are you? Whaddya think about tonight?" As a former player, knowing what he was going through and the pressure he faced, I really respected his initiating the conversation, because he knew I had a job to do, and he had no problems opening up and accommodating me. As we talked, I saw him cutting off about a third of an inch from the knob of his stick. I thought, "A third of an inch? Who does that?" I asked about it and Wayne replied, "My father doesn't think I'm working hard enough. So I'll bend over a little more and it'll force me to work a little harder." I thought that was amazing information. I was blown away! Here was the game's top player, shortly before a big playoff game, realizing I was looking for inside information for my broadcast and providing me with material that would make our show truly unique. PS: He scored two goals that night and Detroit fell in five games.

The Oilers had lost only two of 12 going into the finals against Boston. Gretzky scored the series opening goal, sending the Edmonton crowd into a frenzy as he drifted to a stop behind the net, stick aloft. It was Wayne's spring, his 45 points second only to his 47 in 1985, his 31 assists a new record; and it was Wayne's finals, with 10 assists and 13 points, also a new record.

It was Wayne's world. After the sweep was complete, and the Cup was theirs, he gathered the team around for a photo; he and Messier stared wild-eyed at each other and exchanged a crazy laugh. Yet an hour later, when the building was empty and the celebrations were just getting started in the Oilers' dressing room, the solitary Gretzky cut a forlorn figure, sitting on the players' bench, still in uniform, gazing up at the championship banners, contemplating the setting of his jeweled career.

He was relaxing in a steam bath with Kurri later that evening.

"Wayne told me he might not be coming back," Kurri recalled. "I looked at him like he'd gone crazy."

Despite all they achieved, many still wonder how much more dominant they might have become. Two more Cups? Five? We will never know. But we may never see that type of team again. Coaching, videotape, scouting, systems, the way young players are trained, salaries, free agency—all these things have changed so drastically in the last ten years that it may be impossible to duplicate what Edmonton did.

My opinion is that, as great as they were, four people were the engine that drove that team—Sather, Gretzky, Messier and Kevin Lowe. Coffey, Kurri, Anderson and Fuhr were all great players—and it may be strange for me not to select Fuhr as one of the engine parts, but when you are a goaltender, you don't go out and create the game, the game comes to you. You don't know night to night what your impact will be: Will you have to stop 10 shots or 60? But Slats assembled and molded them, Kevin was the rudder when things got a bit wobbly, Messier was the most complete package imaginable of fierce physical force combined with skill, heart and peer motivation, and Gretzky was the genius, who night after night created more offense than anyone ever had. I don't think it's an insult to any of the others to say that team could not have accomplished all it did without Gretzky. The astronomical numbers tell the story.

When Gretzky was traded on August 9, 1988, Canada went into shock. The deal was front-page news everywhere, including the *New York Times*, but Canadians were righteously outraged. Just days earlier, they had witnessed Wayne on the steps of a cathedral in Edmonton with Janet, his new bride, the central figures in Canada's version of a Royal Wedding. Now he was being exported to Los Angeles, where the sport of hockey wasn't even a blip on the local radar.

In a speech to Parliament, one legislator called Gretzky a "national symbol, like the beaver. How can we allow the sale of our national symbols? The Edmonton Oilers without Wayne Gretzky is like Wheel of Fortune without Vanna White."

For Gretzky, "The Trade," as it became known, meant another complex challenge. The Kings lacked Edmonton's talent and depth. In the celluloid city, their games were mere rumors.

His arrival changed things literally overnight—within 24 hours 2,500 new season tickets were sold. On opening night, against Detroit, Gretzky's sharp angle power-play goal against Greg Stefan (a Brantford teammate in the year he scored 378 goals), his first shot as a King, drew 16,005 fans to their feet and hockey to hipness. He added three assists. After the victory, transplanted Canadians Michael J. Fox and John Candy hobnobbed with him in the dressing room, leading the parade of celebrities who would frequent the Forum over the next few years.

Hundreds of thousands of Angelinos, for whom a line change meant a script revision, suddenly discovered a 21-year-old franchise.

From a business standpoint, The Trade was an immediate bonanza. The Kings' average attendance jumped 3,000 a night and by 1991-92, the entire home schedule was sold out. Kings ticket revenue doubled. Season ticket sales tripled. As a road attraction, club officials claimed the 1987-88 Kings didn't sell out a game. But in Wayne's first season, the Kings played to 30 sellouts.

The estimated value of the franchise tripled over the next five years, the sale of broadcast rights and ad sales doubled and quadrupled respectively. The redesigned uniform, from purple and gold to black, gray and white, became the hottest sports apparel item anywhere.

With hockey mining a mother lode in one Sun Belt city, a gold rush for new markets commenced. Nine new NHL teams sprouted across the South. And minor league hockey exploded, with entire leagues rooted in new markets that had previously had little or no hockey exposure. It amounted to a new map for hockey and there's little question that Gretzky's trade was the catalyst.

A new phenomenon, roller hockey, sprouted in the areas where ice was not readily available. USA Hockey reported a dramatic jump in youth registration. These and other developments would be difficult to envision had Gretzky not been dealt to Los Angeles.

On the ice, the Kings' fortunes rose immediately. Their second-place finish in 1989 was their best in eight seasons and, in a dramatic first round series against Edmonton, Gretzky rallied his new team from a 3–1 deficit to down his old team by winning three straight games. Southern California went crazy, although Gretzky was a touch subdued after sending the Oilers home. "I've got lots of friends in that other room," he said.

The Kings were then swept by Calgary, the eventual Stanley Cup champions.

Emotions and results seesawed with disheartening regularity over the next few years. A fourth-place finish in 1990 was followed by the Kings' first division title in 1991, then an 18-point plunge in 1992. Although Kurri, Coffey, Huddy, Marty McSorley and Mike Krushelnyski would all reunite with Gretzky in L.A. during his time there, the Kings' hopes for the playoff often died in the second round, and often coincided with a Gretzky injury. His desire to win the Cup again intensified after Messier led the Oilers to the title in 1990, and his rejuvenated play culminated in an inspired run in 1993.

When a back injury forced Wayne from the first 39 games of the 1992-93 season, he rushed his rehab and endured the first prolonged slump of his career. There were pronouncements that his sun had set. When the playoffs began, he immediately ran into problems—an injury, again, early in the first round against Calgary, reportedly to his leg. He struggled early in the round but—in a pattern he'd repeat through the Conference Championship—he would battle adversity in early games and lead the Kings with bravura performances late in the series, in the games that mattered most.

Early in the second round, I was working for ESPN and he disclosed to me he had, in fact, injured a rib, which can be one of the most painful injuries a hockey player can have. The medical staff froze it each game and he would shepherd the Kings to the brink. His finest hour may have been in the Conference finals against the Maple Leafs.

L.A. faced elimination in game six, and with a Toronto writer commenting he was playing as if he had "a piano on his back," Gretzky put the Kings on his back, leading Los Angeles in a come-from-behind charge to the Stanley Cup finals with the overtime winner in game six and a hat trick plus an assist to eliminate Toronto in game seven. Wayne has called it the greatest game he ever played in the NHL.

But the exhilaration would not last. Gretzky's starring role in the game one victory over the venerable Canadiens brought L.A. closer still, and they led game two late in the contest. But the old Montreal Forum possessed unseen forces which could reverse the direction of any series. This time, they worked their voodoo on McSorley, whose late game illegal stick penalty ushered in the first of three consecutive overtime wins by *les Canadiens*, pushing the Kings' seesaw again downward. For only the second time in his career, Gretzky watched a Stanley Cup celebration from the other end of the ice, but this five-game loss hurt most deeply. In a matter of days he went from the greatest game he had ever played to the biggest disappointment of his career, and with the battered year finally behind him with no Cup to show for it, he became disconsolate and publicly contemplated retirement.

The Kings never assembled a club of the caliber Wayne had experienced in Edmonton—and, of course, few teams could. He had to carry more weight on his shoulders. Because he wanted so badly to win, I believe he found the differences between the on-ice situations in Edmonton and L.A. frustrating, and he had to make some adjustments to play with a different kind of pressure.

But the Kings' success off the ice became monumentally significant. The irony of Gretzky's career is that his greatest impact as an ambassador, a salesman for the game, came after his very best days as a player. I firmly believe we won't see the full fruits of what Wayne did for this league until the next generation comes along.

In the meantime, although the Kings would never be a championship team, and Gretzky didn't put up the numbers he previously had, he could take solace in the fact that he began establishing new NHL career records while playing in Los Angeles. He had already become the league's all-time assist leader as an Oiler in March 1988. He finished his initial Kings' season as the first player to reach 1,200 assists.

As the 1989-90 campaign began, Gretzky was 13 points shy of Gordie Howe's all-time scoring record of 1,850 points. With a career average of better than two points per game, he figured to need about half a dozen games to catch his hero. He looked at the schedule and saw the Kings in Edmonton, of all places, for the sixth game of the season.

After The Trade, the city fathers of Edmonton had commissioned a statue of Gretzky holding the Cup, to be placed outside Northlands Coliseum. Edmonton would never forget, and neither would he, so before five minutes had elapsed, he tied Gordie with an assist. Then, in the last minute of play, with the Kings trailing by a goal, his back-handed swipe of a bouncing puck past Bill Ranford tied the score and broke the record.

The game was stopped and Wayne's family, Howe and a variety of hockey officials all came out on the ice. Puck, stick and sweater were all presented to the Hockey Hall of Fame. Ever-gracious, Gretzky was handed the microphone and thanked everyone, including the people of Edmonton and the Oilers, who were so much a part of breaking the record. Then play restarted and Gretzky proceeded to defeat the Oilers with a goal in overtime.

Howe's record of 801 NHL career goals would take a little longer to break, but it tumbled in March 1994, when Gretzky one-timed McSorley's cross-ice pass beyond the reach of Vancouver goalie Kirk McLean for 802.

These accomplishments were accompanied by a fame that transcended any ever achieved by a hockey player. Gretzky's commercials for rental cars, pizzas, sporting goods and apparel, soda and consumer electronics brought him widespread recognition, as did his cartoon character in a Saturday morning kids' show. But nothing could make up for missing the playoffs that spring of 1994, just one year after reaching the finals. Never since his turning pro had one of Gretzky's teams failed to qualify, and it coincided with the serious financial and legal problems of Bruce McNall. The Kings' owner had brought Gretzky to L.A., becoming a close friend and business partner in Canadian football and the highly publicized purchase of a rare Honus Wagner baseball card.

All teams go through cycles. It is the way of sports, and the Kings took an especially rapid dive. When they missed the playoffs for a second consecutive year and McNall's troubles forced him to step away from the operation, the glitter dimmed. With the team staggering, attendance stumbling and no quick turnaround imminent, Gretzky and the Kings parted company in February 1996.

A short stay with St. Louis followed, and a chance to create some magic with his friend Brett Hull. With eight goals and 24 points in 18 Blues games, Gretzky used his talents to lift the team and sell out the Kiel Center.

A free agent on July 1, 1996, Gretzky elected to reunite with Mark Messier in New York, where Messier had led the Rangers to the Cup in 1994. Another old friend was Colin Campbell, now Rangers coach. "It would be a mistake for the team, the media and the fans to expect him to be the Wayne Gretzky of 1982 or 1988 or even 1993," said Campbell. "In the major team sports, the Joe Montanas, the Walter Paytons, all the stars have the sun set on them sooner or later. Gretz and Mark are going to be 36 and that's old for team sports. It's the downside of the mountain. We can't expect them to carry the team the same way they did in the past."

The Rangers still had much of the young core of their Cup team, with Brian Leetch, Adam Graves and Alexei Kovalev. And Gretzky formed a good on-ice rapport with young Swedish winger Niklas Sundstrom. The Rangers did not overwhelm the league in the regular season, finishing only four games over .500. But in an age when NHL defenses had tightened up dramatically and goaltenders were becoming the dominant players in the game, Gretzky's league best of 72 assists and fourth-place finish in league scoring drew raves on Broadway.

But, as an old Broadway showman once put it, they hadn't seen nothin' yet. When the playoffs rolled around, Gretzky scored the first goal of game two and added an assist in a shutout over Florida, tying the series at 1-1, then scored all the Rangers' goals with a second-period

Gretzky's trade to Los Angeles in 1988 heralded significant changes in the NHL.

hat trick—the ninth of his Stanley Cup career—in game four, as the Rangers went on to defeat the Panthers in five games.

Against the cross-Hudson River rival New Jersey Devils in Round 2, Gretzky added two more goals and three assists, two of them on game-winning goals, as the Rangers again rebounded from a game one loss to take the series.

The Flyers were up next and again the Rangers dropped the opening game. But Gretzky's 10th career playoff hat trick sparked the Rangers' 5–4 victory to even the series. However, injuries and absences by key players took their toll, and although the Rangers battled gallantly against a bigger, stronger Philadelphia team, they ultimately fell in five games. Gretzky was the Rangers' leading playoff scorer in each round and enjoyed a nine-game scoring streak.

No playoff defeat was ever easy, but this one approached the 1993 loss for being disappointing. "Unfortunately, we ran into two or three injuries and one of the guys on the team had a family member pass away," he said. "I think we had a legitimate chance to make some hay."

Messier departed for Vancouver that summer and the Rangers struggled afterward. They missed the playoffs for two consecutive years and it was a great disappointment for Wayne to be on the sidelines in both his final two seasons. The playoffs are what a hockey player lives for, and I know he was quite unhappy sitting on the sidelines while the Cup was being contested.

It didn't help that the respect Wayne had always been accorded by the opposition in the NHL seemed to be eroding. Young players who came into the league without an appreciation for what he did would rough him up. In the NHL, someone of Gretzky's stature will not be a target for dirty play. The majority of players understand respect and no one has ever deserved that respectful treatment more than Wayne. I think as Gretzky matured as a player and a person, he received more mature treatment from the opposition. Half the guys would watch from the bench just to see what he did—they were in awe of him. And they respected what he'd done for the game, which greatly enhanced what they were doing and how much they were receiving in compensation.

Don't misunderstand me, the NHL remains a very rugged place. Paul Karyia certainly has been leveled, Mario Lemieux may have been chopped more than anyone. People laid off Bobby Orr, but that was because his teammates would kill anyone who tried to cross him. The Bruins were a big-time nasty team, proficient in back-alley tactics. You'd be forced to skate through the stick of Wayne Cashman if you messed with Orr. It was the same thing with Bobby Clarke and the Flyers. It wasn't that players wouldn't try to hit Gretzky—they would if they could. But if they caught him, they wouldn't head-hunt, they wouldn't put an elbow through his ear or take the opportunity to slash him across the wrist. Wayne was checked all right, but he was very rarely hammered. It was the same when I played against Gordie Howe during his last NHL season. He was lumbering around the ice in his fifties. As an opposition player, you ask yourself, "Do I try to run him? This guy's a legend." Of course, with Gordie, if you did, you might have ended up with a Sher-wood sandwich.

Pro-Stars cartoon, 1992. Wayne is flanked by Michael Jordan (left) and Bo Jackson.

Vaclav Varada, from Buffalo, was particularly tough on Gretz in his last season. Although so many players from both sides of the Atlantic grew up with Gretzky posters on their walls, it's possible that Varada may not have had an understanding of what Wayne brought to hockey, how he broke down barriers. Bill Muckalt, a rookie from Vancouver, also delivered a questionable hit on him. Suddenly, here kids were lining up against him, thinking, "Well, he doesn't look so good. I'm gonna hit him." You could understand their point: They were trying to earn a position—and if they did, they'd make a wonderful living because of what Wayne did in helping raise the profile of the sport and player salaries. But younger players didn't see and couldn't appreciate all of what Wayne accomplished, so the respect was perhaps fading. On the Gretzky time line, the end seemed to be at hand.

So there was some pain down the stretch. There was the pain of losing; Wayne hated not scoring more goals or points; he was hurt and had to take cortisone injections on a few occasions. Those shots were not fun. Mike Richter said it best when he told the *New York Times*, "Maturing throughout your career is insidious. Quietly, it starts to put limitations on what you're able to do. Wayne sees the game probably better now than ever. But it's a cruelty of sports that when you're mentally at your peak, you start to deteriorate physically. He has so much willpower that he overcomes whatever level of deterioration his body has had." Nevertheless Gretzky truly enjoyed New York and his final

stop as a Ranger left us with some great memories. He led the team in scoring, added to his career scoring totals and set new records that may never be matched.

On March 7, 1998, Wayne scored his 1,000th NHL career goal—regular season and play-offs—against New Jersey. A few weeks later, against Detroit, he got his 1,900th regular-season assist.

He became the leading scorer in NHL All-Star Game history with two assists, including one on the game winner in 1998. But that was just a prelude for his MVP performance, the third time he won the award, in the 1999 All-Star Game in Tampa. Playing on a line with Theo Fleury and Mark Recchi, he tallied a goal and two marvelous assists and so dominated play that, at one point in the third period, fellow All-Stars on the benches stood and applauded him.

He enjoyed that game immensely and I probably should have realized he was contemplating retirement that day. He relished the whole experience, spending time with fellow players and people around the game, sitting back and watching people's reactions to various goings-on, shaking hands, talking to people, saving sticks. He acted that way the entire last few weeks.

And he kept the truck he won as the All-Star MVP. He had given away all the other cars and trucks he had won, and there were plenty of them. But this time, he didn't. "After 21 years of pro hockey, 20 in the NHL, I just feel like this is the one thing I want to keep," Gretzky said that day, the day before his 38th birthday. "It's kind of like a trophy to me. I want to have it and I want to remember it."

One of Gretzky's most incredible statistical achievements is that he registered 96 games in which he scored five or more points. But none to me was more memorable and amazing than his first trip to Nashville about three weeks after the 1999 All-Star Game. The atmosphere in the building was electric (and it's one of those places where hockey might not have gotten a chance to grab a foothold had it not been for Gretzky's tenure in Los Angeles).

The Predators have an entertaining, quick team and the fans really enjoy themselves, but this night was special. Halfway through the game the Rangers were leading 6–0 and Gretzky was really putting on a show. He had four assists and on one, with no apparent options for passing on the power play, he elected to bank the puck off the goal frame right to Kevin Stevens, who scored the goal. In almost any arena, if the home team falls behind 6–0, the crowd goes home. Instead, the place went absolutely nuts because of Gretzky's performance. Then Nashville scored three goals, live country music was being performed in the aisles of the arena and what should have been a frustrating night for the fans became a real party. Gretzky added another assist and the Rangers held on to win the game. I think he realized this would be his only trip ever to Nashville and he wanted to put his stamp on the game, something people there would always remember. And he did.

Traveling with Gretzky during the three years he played in New York provided me with a different kind of view of him. We generally sat across the aisle from each other on airplanes. It's no secret that he is not a good flier. He was quick to recognize changes in the weather and at the first indication of a bumpy ride, he'd unfasten his seat belt and go visit the pilots, which you can do on charter flights. It seemed to give him a sense of relief to know what was going on in the cockpit.

Most other players get on planes and play cards or read books and newspapers. More recently, you see players plugging in their computers and checking out various aspects of the business world. But Gretzky came on the plane and immediately began inquiring about what was going on in hockey. He'd talk about last night's games or how long a suspension the NHL might give a particular player. And we'd debate these things. We'd rate players and coaches, we'd go over the fine points of hockey, talk about certain Canada Cup games. We'd talk about styles of teams, why one player was successful and another was not, why one coach had certain problems and how other coaches dealt with them. I would often wait for him to get on the plane and sit down just so I could tell him the latest gossip or news about impending trades; he'd get on board and I'd say, "I've got a scoop," and tell him So-and-So was about to be traded and he'd say, "Oh, I heard that two days ago." It was hard to out-scoop the guy. He was plugged in really well. Once in a while, he'd sit down and tell me about impending trades that he had made up just to test my reaction. He had a lot of fun with those.

It was clear he watched a lot of hockey on TV via satellite. You would think that with his time constraints he might not be able to watch so much hockey, or that he would like to just put it aside once in a while. Instead, he made it a priority. He didn't seem to want to get away from it. Hockey has been his passion from the very beginning.

It was also fascinating to watch him interact with his teammates, who really liked him, which is quite unique for an athlete of his stature. When the Rangers came into Ottawa for his last game in Canada, the Senators' Bill Berg, who played with Wayne in New York for two seasons, said in an interview, "He's the kind of guy you want your kids to become when they grow up, and not just because of what he's accomplished, because he's a genuine good person." This is the overwhelming view of those who know him.

The place where that affection was best observed was at practices. When you play hockey for a living, the one place that is yours—your world—is at practice with your teammates, the guys you live with for nine or ten months of every year. Each team is its own society and its own government. Different people have different roles. Some function as leaders, some are comedians, some are leaders because they are comedians. Each time a player goes into the dressing room, whether he's getting his ankle taped in the medical room or just schmoozing with the boys over coffee at 9:00 a.m., or on the ice, he feels something special. As soon as practice ends, he must face all manner of outside situations about which he may not feel completely comfortable, because being a hockey player has been one of life's few constants since he was a child. The rink is where he feels most at ease. And in the dressing room and at practice, Wayne was fun to be around, a real cut-up, throwing around one-liners and zingers with the best of them. When the situation permitted, he'd have fun by creating conditions on the ice to keep everyone loose.

For years, in every NHL city, when Gretzky arrived at an arena, one thing was certain: A mountain of objects to be autographed would await him in the dressing room. A lot of it was for players on the opposition, sometimes for the opposition's former players, who would come to the arena because they had a charity golf tournament or dinner or some other fundraising event. Wayne's autograph on a picture or stick or puck or sweater commands a very hefty donation. I don't believe one can begin to estimate the amount of money contributed from these items to charity auctions, tennis tournaments and functions of that nature. It could be tens of millions of dollars. The Rangers had one trip in 1999 which took them to Tampa Bay, Miami, Carolina and Pittsburgh in five nights—and, inevitably, the first thing we'd see in each dressing room was that mountain for Wayne to sign.

That same road trip featured Gretzky in another of his roles, that of hockey ambassador. Wayne left the plane in Raleigh-Durham about 6:00 p.m. and immediately went, on behalf of the Hurricanes, to a press conference publicizing the fact that he was in town. He did two TV interviews and a few more for radio and the next day there was a big story in the local paper about him. That night, over 19,000 fans showed up in an arena where they don't often get half that number, all because Wayne took two hours to publicize the game. A lot of guys who had just played back-to-back games would not have done that. They would prefer to go out for dinner or see a movie. But a lot of guys are not Wayne Gretzky.

In his early years, Wayne was known in the media as a very polite interview, but he offered mostly cliches. Hockey players have historically been the most accommodating, polite, media-friendly athletes. Some of that came from their upbringing, and some from a desire to do everything they could to help promote hockey. It resulted in Gretzky's uncertainty about the proper ways and times to express his true feelings. When he did venture an unusual opinion (such as the night he called the New Jersey Devils a "Mickey Mouse organization" when he felt bad for their goaltenders after he scored three goals and added five assists in a 13–4 Edmonton drubbing), it sometimes got him into trouble. But increasingly, as he matured, his answers became far more perceptive and extremely thoughtful. More often, later in his career, he stood up for his beliefs.

In recent years, the remarkable leap in media demand has fostered unprecedented competition. More suburban papers cover sports, sports talk radio stations have proliferated, network cable TV has grown, local cable coverage is becoming more of a factor and now there are websites with their own correspondents. The media's demands on an athlete when Wayne started playing were completely unlike what they are today.

As almost any writer or reporter will attest, Wayne has been incredibly friendly with the media since the beginning; on only the rarest of occasions was he not a willing interview—day in, day out, win or lose for 21 professional seasons, playoffs, international tournaments, after practices and every other situation imaginable. He set a strong example for the rest of the league, and players understand today that increased media attention might lead to opportunities for them in the marketplace. The NHL would do well to produce a training video with Wayne for its players on cooperating with the media and the rewards that might come from it.

Gretzky has always maintained that everything he has, everything he's become, came from hockey, and he has taken great pains to show respect and generosity to those who have helped him along the way. He is not selfish with the rewards of his fame. The Rangers played in Florida during baseball's spring training and he visited Baltimore's camp, taking some of the team's public relations and front office personnel with him to the ballpark to meet Orioles ironman Cal Ripken.

When teams flew into Los Angeles, it wasn't unusual for Wayne to have set some players up for a round of golf at his course. Imagine Rocky Smith of the St. Louis Blues home for the summer telling his friends, "Yeah, I was in L.A. and played Gretzky's course—and he paid for it." He recognized these things meant a lot to people who might not otherwise have that opportunity on their own. But he got enjoyment out of making others feel special and bringing them into his world.

This is just one story of thousands: I arranged for Wayne to play golf at a course where the club superintendent is a friend of mine. After Wayne played, he stopped at the superintendent's house, which is on the course, and signed some hockey cards for his children. The following day, on his way to the airport, he stopped by the house with two signed sticks for the family, having made sure to remember the kids' names so that the autographs were personalized.

Even on the biggest day of the season, the day he played his final game, he displayed incredible consideration. While driving to the Garden, he phoned me to say he felt terrible because, in all the excitement of the last few days, in which he had thanked so many people, he had neglected to thank two in particular—Dan Kelly and Tom Mees, two great hockey announcers who had passed away. He asked if I could relay that information during the telecast, which I did. Both the Kelly and Mees families were incredibly appreciative of that gesture.

In a sense, Wayne was only giving back what hockey had given him. In the last few weeks of his career, hockey fans who may have been hard on him over time (after all, he had come into their arenas and beaten their teams for years) displayed the greatest affection toward him, in tribute to what he did for the game we all love.

For example, in February 1999, the Rangers visited Calgary and the fans recognized it would likely be Gretzky's final visit. They cheered his every shift and with two minutes remaining and the Flames well in the lead, the crowd gave him a standing ovation and chanted his name so forcefully that Fleury told the press afterwards, "I'm surprised they didn't boo us." He was holding one of Gretzky's sticks as he spoke. Over time, Calgarians had grown to respect and even love Gretzky. Some of that can be attributed to the Olympics, in which he represented Canada so well, even though the team did not win. Wayne had played well, had stayed in the Olympic Village and gone to watch other Canadian athletes compete, and that resonated with Calgarians and Canadians, who recognized he didn't consider himself to be superior. In addition, when Gretzky moved to L.A., he remained a Canadian, coming home for his charity tennis tournament or his father's golf tournament, representing Canada in international hockey. Canada is a passionate country. They love their game and feel it slipping away at times. But here was the world's greatest player who, despite the fact that he might play golf in L.A. with Jack Nicholson, never forgot his roots.

The Calgary fans brought Wayne to tears. He hadn't played well and it had been a rough game. He exited the Saddledome following the game, with the Rangers' no-nonsense security man Dennis Ryan at his side, hustling him to the bus and perhaps 3,000 fans waiting outside to get a final glimpse of him. Suddenly Wayne said, "Hold it," and for the next 25 minutes he autographed photos, posters, signs, everything handed to him. He could have been there for three hours. He would not have been faulted for jumping on the team bus instead, but Gretzky knows that any autograph he gives will be framed and hung in a youngster's room, representing the mutual respect between the people in hockey and the fans.

In April 1999, Wayne received another tribute, this time from the Chicago fans. The Hawks were dominating the Rangers in one of the last games of the season and with a few minutes remaining in the game, Gretzky's picture appeared on the video scoreboard. Seemingly out of nowhere, the crowd in United Center erupted in cheers for a player they had regularly booed since he had dismantled the Blackhawks in the playoffs 15 years earlier.

That night the flight from Chicago to Dallas had a frightening takeoff after we had been on the runway for hours. I could sense that his discomfort with air travel, the fatigue and injuries had all taken their toll. He mentioned to me during the flight that he was thinking about leaving the game. By that time, Gretzky was using at least four sticks nightly, and he was marking each one. The trainers told me he had also been collecting mementos. I had begun to put things together, and the next night in Dallas, I said on the air that Wayne just might be considering retirement. Then I saw Guy Carbonneau walk out of the arena with one of Gretzky's sticks and I felt I should talk to Wayne. I told him what I had said on the air and he replied, "I don't have a problem with that."

The media had speculated on his retirement at least since the All-Star Game, but most concluded that he'd play one more season. The next day was Saturday so I taped a segment for "Hockey Night in Canada," and gave fans a heads-up that when the Rangers played in Ottawa the following week, it might be Gretzky's last NHL game in a Canadian arena. I wanted people to be aware of it. Can you imagine what the reaction would be if the greatest player in the history of the game just walked away? I knew he had said he didn't want a farewell tour, didn't want the attention, so I knew he was capable of

just slipping from the scene.

Nevertheless, I still felt a bit funny about it, so I phoned him again. I never asked him point-blank if he was quitting—I didn't think it was appropriate—but I told him what I had reported and he repeated that it caused him no problems. So on Sunday, I was even more certain of my remarks on the Fox telecast.

The story took off like wildfire. On Monday, when the Rangers played Tampa Bay, an atmosphere of near panic set in. Players, NHL people, fans, media had all grown up with Wayne as part of the scene. After more than two decades, they all seemed upset at the prospect of envisioning a hockey world minus Gretzky. We later learned that Wayne had been discussing retirement with Janet—his soulmate and confidante—since his last trip to Edmonton and Calgary, after which he returned so badly injured that he had to miss his first games since joining the Rangers. But he had declined to make his thinking public for fear it would distract from the Rangers' attempt at gaining a playoff spot, which by now had failed.

On Tuesday, Gretzky informed the Rangers what he was thinking. Reporters who staked out coach John Muckler's office at the Rangers' Rye, NY, practice facility knew Gretzky and Muckler were meeting. Muckler, who had been his assistant coach in Edmonton and was an old friend of Walter Gretzky, tried to persuade Wayne to play one

Gretzky finished tied for the lead in regular-season assists in 1996-97 and 1997-98, his first two seasons in New York.

more year. The reporters guessed the outcome when they saw Muckler overcome with emotion afterward.

By the time we hit Ottawa on Thursday night, the reality had set in, although no official announcement had been made. The Senators were fighting for the Conference Championship but—with Walter, Phyllis, Janet and his children at the Corel Centre—cheers erupted each time Gretzky touched the puck. By the 2–2 game's conclusion, the crowd had long been on its feet in thundering tribute. After the siren, the Senators came over, one by one, to shake his hand. Senators defenseman Lance Pitlick blamed Gretzky for an epidemic of sore necks among Senators blueliners over the years, thanks to Wayne lasering pucks past them. As Pitlick shook hands (hoping, he said, that "some of the greatness would rub off") he warned Gretzky, "This is your last chance to get one of my sticks."

Three times Gretzky tried to leave the ice; three times he had to return to acknowledge the Ottawa crowd, which thanked him on behalf of his country. At the packed press conference afterward, Gretzky said all indications pointed to him deciding to retire although he had not finalized the

did, but it's not a perfect world… It's not going to happen that way, not this year, but it is nice to be able to say people do want me to play more."

"As I said to John (Muckler) on Tuesday, I want to be remembered—especially by him and by hockey fans everywhere—as a player who always could make a strong contribution to the team in important situations. And that's why it's time for me to leave now."

When Sunday afternoon arrived, "99" was painted on the ice behind each net. Thousands of fans wore "99" sweaters in the stands—a number that will never be worn again by an NHL player. In addition to his family, the pregame ceremony included Sather, who gave Gretzky a bear hug; Lemieux, who Gretzky called "the best player I ever played against;" and wearing sunglasses, "the greatest I ever played with"—Mark Messier. "I was ecstatic when I heard he was coming. It was great to be on the ice with him again," Gretzky said later. "He came to New York and showed people how to handle pressure."

Rock star Bryan Adams sang "Oh, Canada," and substituted "We're gonna miss you, Wayne Gretzky" for "We stand on guard for thee."

John Amirante amended the "Star Spangled Banner" substituting "the land of Wayne Gretzky" for "the land of the free."

The Pittsburgh Penguins provided the opposition. In typical fashion Gretzky set up shop over the "99" at the Eighth Avenue end of the rink and fed several passes to teammates that, unfortunately, failed to click. He took a few shots that just sailed wide. Gordie Howe appeared via video on the scoreboard to offer his best wishes. In the second period, Michael Jordan materialized on the scoreboard, and after a couple of opportunities with

Top awards in different spheres: Left: with editor Steve Dryden as #99 is ranked #1 in the Hockey News Top 50 NHL Players of All-Time. Right: receiving the Order of Canada from Governor-General Romeo Leblanc.

decision. He also apologized to the Senators for bringing the spectacle of a clamoring media to town as they battled for first place.

The next day, he surprised no one at another packed press conference when he said, "This is a party, this is a celebration. I hope everyone understands that I look upon these next few days as something to really enjoy. It's obvious today that I've officially retired and Sunday will be my last game." Then his eyes moistened and his voice caught. "I guess I should take my own advice, huh?"

"My heart, my gut, tell me it's the right time," he explained. "I started to feel fatigue—mentally and physically—that I never felt before. I started questioning myself about it… Everybody wants to go out like Michael Jordan

linemate John MacLean just missed connecting, his old linemate Kovalev, now a Penguin, gave Pittsburgh the lead. But as the period ended, Gretzky fed the puck back to the point on the power play to Matt Schneider, who faked a shot, then drilled a pass to Leetch, standing alone outside the crease. His shot was redirected by behind Tom Barrasso to tie the game. The Garden nearly moved off its foundations as the crowd chanted his name. For Gretzky, it would be his final statistic, his 1,963rd assist and 2,857th point in the NHL.

In the Rangers' dressing room during the second intermission, Gretzky gave one of his rare speeches, and then gave each player, coach and member of the training staff one of his sticks, signed and dated in appreciation for their friendship and support during his time in New York.

A few more opportunities materialized in the final period, but none found the mark. With 40 seconds remaining, Muckler called a timeout and the Garden again rose to its feet in tribute. Muckler, whose daughter had given birth that day, called Gretzky to the bench and told him, "'I just had a grandson today and you've got to get the winner."

"Maybe when I was younger I might have got the winner for him," he'd say later. "I didn't get it for him today and I know it's the right time."

It was Pittsburgh's Jaromir Jagr, Gretzky's choice as "the best young player in the game today," who beat Richter for the game winner shortly into overtime, a goal Gretzky said was "fitting." As the teams shook hands, Jagr told Gretzky, "I didn't mean to do it."

"That's what I used to say," Gretzky replied.

A video tribute followed, then Gretzky took a number of slow turns around the ice, waving at fans, acknowledging friends. Many of his former teammates were in attendance, including Coffey and Anderson, and Wayne later admitted to getting choked up when he saw Ulf Samuelsson, who had become a good friend and was traded to Detroit a few weeks earlier.

The Rangers joined him for a lap around, applauding him all the while, then gathering around for an on-ice picture, as Gretzky used to do whenever the Oilers won a championship.

He left, he returned, and left again. The ovation and the thanks stretched into the early evening.

He met the press for one last time, a long, warm session that ended in spontaneous applause. Then he began his new life.

One of the first things he did was to accept an invitation from Glen Sather to visit Edmonton during the playoffs. When you consider what he went through down the stretch, the international media attention, the pressure of making the decision, it was one more thing no one would have faulted him for not doing. He didn't have to go to Edmonton, but he wanted to give the fans there a chance to say thanks and goodbye and to do the same himself.

For the next while, I'm sure Wayne will enjoy spending more time with his family. He remains an attractive spokesman for corporations and he has cemented some very interesting business relationships that will enable him to remain closer to home with Janet and his children.

But hockey has been Wayne's life and he has always been and remains deeply concerned about its direction and future. I can't imagine him serving as a "yes-man" for the NHL. Instead I can see him becoming involved at the ownership level of an NHL franchise with a voice on the NHL's Board of Governors. Think about how familiar he is with so many aspects of the game—from the training staff to the game on the ice to the playing rules—even to the right way to stage an on-ice ceremony—after all, who has been involved in more? Then add what he can contribute after having played in a small Canadian market and large U.S. markets. Plus he has learned a great deal being involved in the corporate world. He has an understanding of both sides of player-ownership questions. He's been a visible, active spokesman in selling the game, and is a strong advocate for youth hockey. He is bright and has amazing common sense. He is a man who could be a strong leader for a franchise and an amazing resource for the game's future.

Given what we've seen of Wayne Gretzky since he first stepped onto the ice, I don't think he'll be away from the game for long. New challenges will surely beckon.

With wife Janet, Paulina, Ty and Trevor, New York City, 1999.

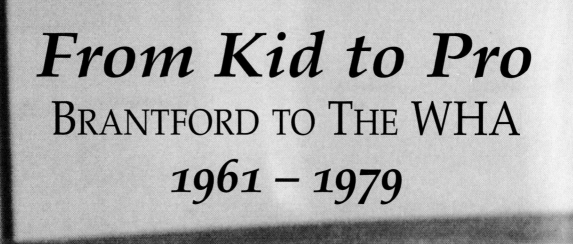

From Kid to Pro

BRANTFORD TO THE WHA

1961 – 1979

Wayne Gretzky of the Vaughan Nationals
versus the Bramalea Blues, Ontario
Hockey Association Junior B, 1975.

99 *Opposite:* You can see by the crease marks that I hadn't worn the pants for a while, but these are the slacks and the sports jacket I would wear for church. I'm five years old here. The pellet gun is my grandmother's. The beret I have on is my grandfather's marching hat. He was very proud of having been a Canadian soldier so this was the hat he always wore on Remembrance Day. The medals are his from World War I and I still have them today. *Above:* This picture was taken when I was 10. I believe it was at the hockey tournament where I scored 50 goals in nine games. One of the papers wanted a picture of my dad *(Walter)* and me, and this was the picture they took.

99 This is my first goal right here. My very first goal. Top corner, over the glove, or at least that's how I remember it! I was six years old. It was against a team from the city of Stratford.

99 My uncle Bob Hockin coached me the year I got 378 goals. My dad had coached me for three years before that year, but he said, "I better not coach because of all the ice time you're going to get." He never coached me again on an organized team. The goalie on our team that year was Greg Stefan. (The name on the back of his sweater is our team name, Steelers.) Len Hachborn was the assistant captain. Len and Greg both played in the NHL. The guy between Len and my uncle is Jim Burton. He played in the International League and in Europe.

99 *Opposite:* That's my dad shoveling off the rink in our backyard. He was always proud of the rink. In the summer, he never used to hose down the lawn. People were always so mad because he had the greenest grass. It was from all the snow and ice that had melted since wintertime.

Ingersol, Ontario, tournament champions, 1969. Wayne is in the bottom row, third from the left. Walter is in the top row, far right.

99 *Left:* Look at that long hair! We look like an all-girls team. I'm in the middle of the bottom row in this picture taken in 1973. I was a pitcher and shortstop. Funny thing is, it's all the same guys again. That's Jim Burton to my far right, then Greg Stefan and Len Hachborn. I think that my brother Keith is the little guy to my left. I know the other kid is Greg's brother, Joe.

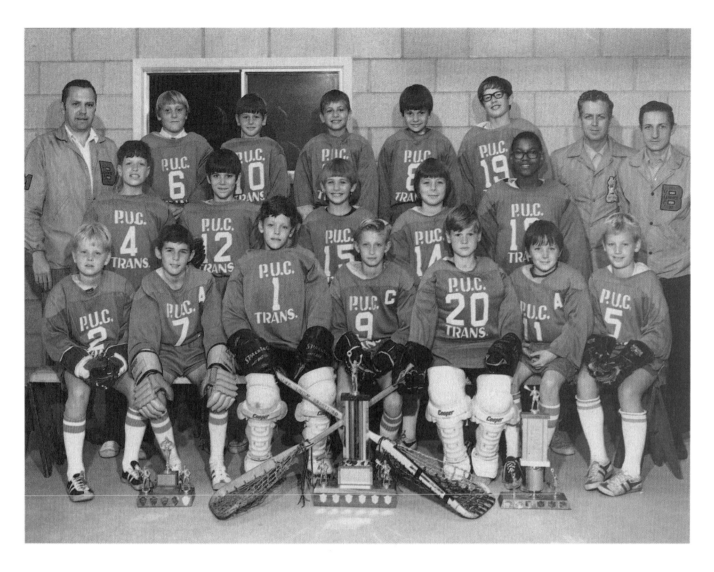

99 The biggest influence in my hockey career was the fact that I played lacrosse (*#9, above*). That's where I learned to protect myself from hard body checks. In those days you could be hit from behind in lacrosse, as well as cross checked, so you had to learn how to roll body checks for self-protection. I scored a lot as a lacrosse player, but not as much as I did in hockey. My father (*top row, right*) was always the team's assistant coach. He drove me to every game and practice, so the head coaches knew they could always count on him.

Combined hockey and lacrosse photo appeared in the program of a sports celebrity dinner to demonstrate that Wayne was a year-round athlete.

99 *Above, wearing captain's "C":* You can see by the angle of my right hand that I don't have any laces in my gloves. I always took them out. That was because I saw that Bobby Orr didn't use laces.

At left: My relationship with Gordie Howe began the day this picture was taken. *(May 4, 1972 at the Kiwanis Great Men of Sports Dinner in Brantford.)* Obviously I was very nervous. A lot of times when people meet their idols they get disappointed, but our meeting turned out to be bigger and better than I ever dreamed. It was such a great moment for me. After that, I would see him from time to time. I played Junior B hockey with his son Murray, and later I played with and against Gordie in some all-star games. We have a relationship that's really fun and have had a lot of good times together.

Wayne Gretzky's Early Milestones

- 100th career goal, January 1, 1970 vs. Hespeler.
- Member of Brantford PUC Transport Lacrosse, city champions, 1972. Gretzky's season statistics: 31 games played, 158 goals, 66 assists, 224 points.
- 50 goals in nine games at Hespeler Ontario Hockey Tournament, 1971-72.
- Gretzky attracts record crowds at Golden Horseshoe Hockey Tournament 1972. 36,000 fans attended.
- First Canadian national magazine coverage appeared in the Star Weekly, April, 1972.
- Member of Canadian national champion Beaver League baseball team, 1972.
- Played with Brantford Turkstra Lumber at 15th annual Quebec PeeWee Hockey Tournament, February 1974: Game one – Brantford 25, Richardson (Texas) 0 (Gretzky had 7 goals, 4 assists); game two – Brantford 9, Beaconsfield (Quebec) 1 (2 goals, 3 assists); game three – Brantford 7, Verdun (Quebec) 3 (3 goals, 3 assists); game four – Oshawa (Ontario) 9, Brantford 4 (1 goal, 3 assists). Tournament total: 4 games, 13 goals, 13 assists, 26 points. Wayne's white gloves earned him the nickname "The White Tornado" at this event.
- 1000th career goal, April 10, 1974. Brantford 8, Waterford 1.
- Leading scorer, Humber Collegiate basketball team, 1977 City champions. Averaged 20.1 points-per-game.

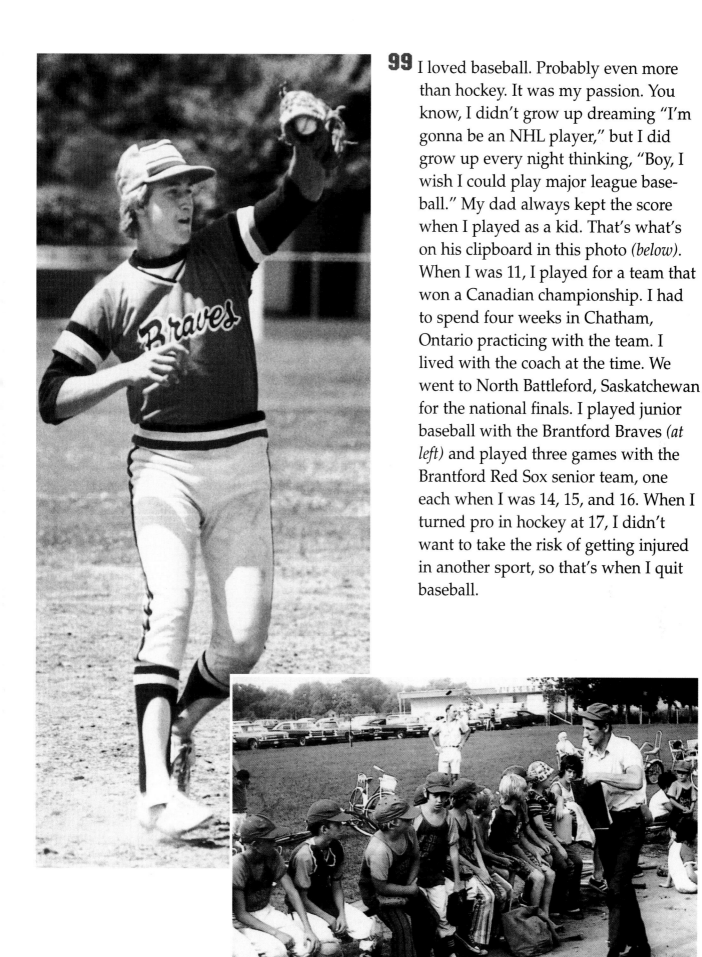

99 I loved baseball. Probably even more than hockey. It was my passion. You know, I didn't grow up dreaming "I'm gonna be an NHL player," but I did grow up every night thinking, "Boy, I wish I could play major league base-ball." My dad always kept the score when I played as a kid. That's what's on his clipboard in this photo *(below)*. When I was 11, I played for a team that won a Canadian championship. I had to spend four weeks in Chatham, Ontario practicing with the team. I lived with the coach at the time. We went to North Battleford, Saskatchewan for the national finals. I played junior baseball with the Brantford Braves *(at left)* and played three games with the Brantford Red Sox senior team, one each when I was 14, 15, and 16. When I turned pro in hockey at 17, I didn't want to take the risk of getting injured in another sport, so that's when I quit baseball.

Above: Pitching 1972; Left: third from left at a
hockey tournament in Goderich, Ontario, 1974.

Phyllis with crests and pennants.

The trophy room. From left: Walter, Brent, Phyllis, Glenn, Kim, Keith.

99 The house that I grew up in *(opposite bottom)* is like a tour spot now. My dad still brings people in to look at things. That's a part of his life that he really loves. He's honestly very proud of it, but I think he has even more fun watching the kids' expressions when they get a chance to come through. He's really excited for them, and he loves the fact that he can be a part of their whole evening. My mom *(Phyllis)* is the opposite. She would go upstairs when everyone comes in. She always stayed in the background. Nowadays, I see my dad a lot and talk to him often, but it's my mom I talk to almost every day. She's the one I talk to one-on-one. I think all the kids in our family communicate with her in a way that doesn't get a lot of attention—and we probably all like it better that way.

Vaughan Nationals, 1975-76. Gretzky is in the middle row, fourth from the left.

99 *Opposite:* This picture was taken when I was living with the Cornish family in Toronto. I think Billy Cornish made me wear the hat. It might have been Dominion Day *(July 1)*, 1976.

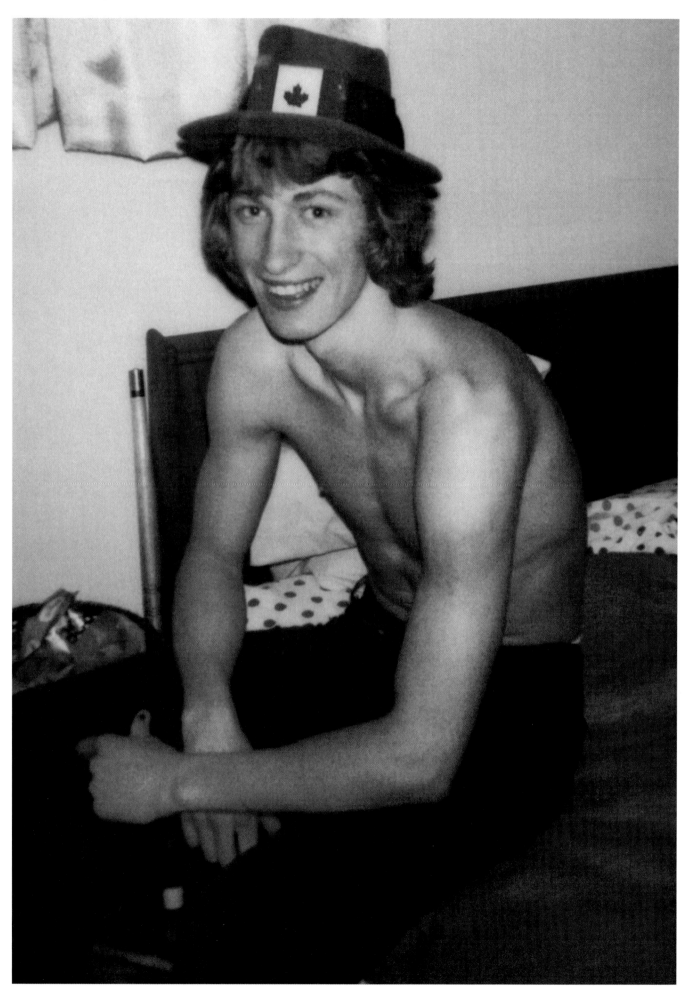

I was going into grade nine when I came to Toronto in 1975. It was great to be treated as just one of the kids in school. Brian Mizzi was my closest friend in high school in Toronto. That's him *(at left, on the far right)* beside Bill Cornish and me. My arm is around Monique Agostino, Billy's girlfriend at the time. Living with Billy turned out to be great for me. He was a really assertive guy. Very outgoing and not bashful whatsoever. When I went to live with his family in Toronto I was really shy and quiet. He helped me grow up and not be intimidated by people. He played a huge part in my being able to deal with crowds and the media.

Keith Gretzky, Kim Gretzky, Wayne Gretzky, Bill Cornish

Canada:

The Judicial District of York   **Province of Ontario**

In Her Majesty's Surrogate Court of the County of York

No. 3850/75

BE IT KNOWN that on the 19th day of June in the year of our Lord one thousand nine hundred and seventy-five

WILLIAM CORNISH, Purchasing Agent and RHETA CORNISH, Sales Woman, both of the Borough of Etobicoke in the County of Judicial District of York were / appointed Guardians of the person only of

WAYNE D. GRETZKY

the infant child of WALTER GRETZKY, Bell Canada/ Employee and PHYLLIS GRETZKY, Housewife, both of the Village of Brantford in the County of County of Brant and Letters of Guardianship are accordingly granted by the said Court to the said WILLIAM & RHETA CORNISH with power and authority to them to do all such acts, matters and things as a guardian may or ought to do, under and by virtue of any Act of the Legislature of Ontario, relating to minors and their they the said Walter and Phyllis Gretzky having been duly sworn to faithfully perform the trust of guardianship.

WITNESS His Honour FARQUHAR JOHN MacRAE , Judge of the said Court.

By the Court

H. B. Ridout
H. B. RIDOUT, Registrar.

The notion of a child being sent away from home in order to play against better hockey competition made Wayne's transfer from Brantford to Toronto national news in Canada. The actual story was more complex than this; Wayne's scoring feats in Brantford upset the competitive balance of the local league and made the Gretzkys unpopular with some. In order for Wayne to play hockey in Toronto, it was necessary for him to establish residence there. To this end minor hockey coach Bill Cornish, Sr. and his wife Rheta officially became Wayne's legal guardians. This court document formalized the arrangement, June 19, 1975.

99 Gordie's son Murray Howe was a teammate of mine with the Seneca Nationals in 1976-77. He's the shorter guy in the back row behind the assistant captain. I'm second from the left in the front row. Stu Smith, the tall kid in the second row just behind me, played a little while for the Hartford Whalers in the 1980s. The guy right in the middle of the back row is Daryl Evans, who played for the L.A. Kings. Billy Gardner, who went on to play for Chicago and Hartford, is the assistant captain in the front row. During my stay in Toronto, I also played in the Metro Junior B all-star game *(below)*.

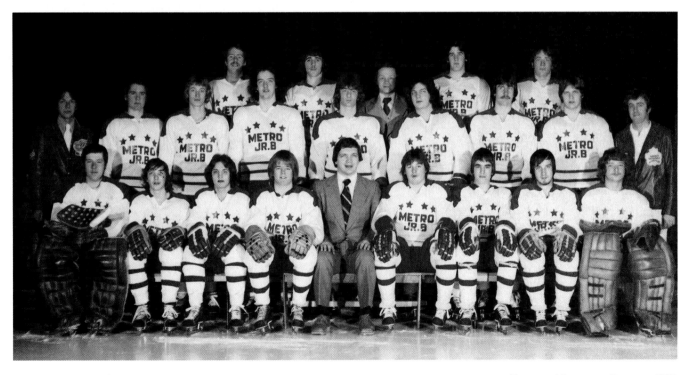

Dear Cornish's:

Hi! How are you? I'm just feeling great up here, but I kind of miss Toronto.

We have been on the ice twice a day for 3 hours in the morning & 3 hours in the afternoon. The fans up here are just super. My right winger played on the Western all-stars in major "A" last year against the Russian juniors. They have decided to let me wear number 99.

How's Billy's job coming along.

When you write back let me know please.

When you come up on the 24th with my father, you brothers can stay here with us.

Sincerely Yours

Wayne

99 Except for my first year, when I wore 11, I wore number 9 all through minor hockey. I couldn't get it in Sault Ste. Marie *(it was worn by Brian Gualazzi)*, so I started with number 14. I kept telling Muzz McPherson *(the general manager)* I wanted to wear 19, but he said "Well, why don't you just wear two 9's?" I said, "Great! I'll take it. "And that's how I got number 99.

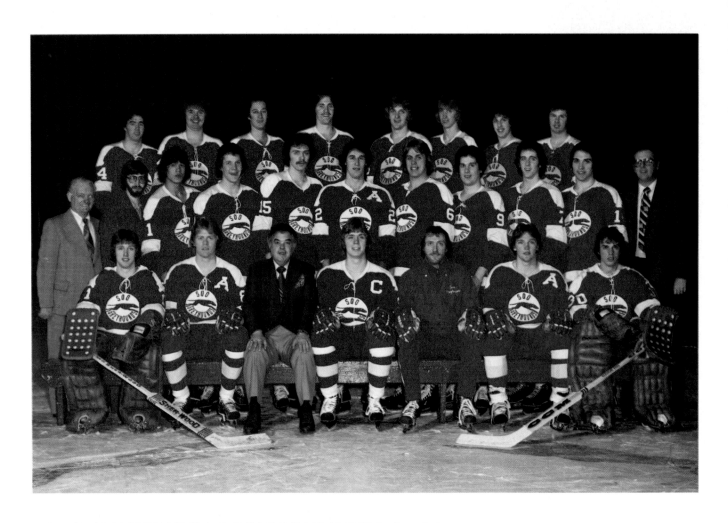

99 *Above:* Craig Hartsburg was the captain when I was in Sault Ste. Marie. Greg Millen is the left-handed goalie. Ted Nolan is in the second row on the left, the first guy in uniform. My line-mates were both assistant captains, Paul Mancini (middle row) and Dan Lucas (front row, left). *Opposite:* I think they had a stick there for this picture. Look at the knob. I would never use a knob like that.

99 The 1978 Ontario Junior A all-star game was played in Windsor. I had three goals. Jimmy Fox was my linemate. He went on to play nine years in Los Angeles where we ended up as teammates on the Kings.

99 The World Junior Championship in 1978 was the first time I ever played against the Russians. They beat us 3–2 at the Quebec Colisee. I was so young at the time—just 16—that I was like a fan. This was the first time I saw the KLM Line (Vladimir Krutov, Igor Larionov and Sergei Makarov). It was also the first time I ever heard of Viacheslav Fetisov (#3, *at left*). He was 20 years old.

99 We earned a bronze medal at the World Juniors, and I think we had 14 guys make the NHL from that team. The guys with me are Pat Riggin (left) and Mike Gartner.

99 Team Canada juniors with the CCM skates on. High off the ice and lots of blade. CCM gloves, stick and helmet too. There must have been a deal.

99 My time with Indianapolis was like a blink of the eye. I got there in June and they had me come back in July to start promoting and selling tickets. They gave me a sweater, it was Blaine Stoughton's, and gloves for this photo shoot. Those aren't even my skates. I would go out to a shopping mall to do promotion and 10 people would show up over the course of four hours. I just used to shake my head. I didn't know what was going on. But then we started the exhibition games, and they were actually kind of fun. We were drawing 9,000-10,000 people a game. Later Nelson Skalbania called me and he said "I'm losing too much money, I gotta trade you. Do you want to go to Winnipeg or Edmonton?" At that time my agent was Gus Badali. I called him and Gus said to tell Skalbania I wanted to go to Edmonton because they had a better chance of getting into the NHL. And that's how I ended up an Oiler.

99 I started wearing a Jofa helmet when I joined the Oilers. All the guys on the team there used them and they said if you're going to play on this team you've got to wear one. Some of the guys actually encouraged me not to wear a helmet at all, so I was a little bit intimidated. I went as far as switching to the Jofa helmet, and that's what I stuck with.

Hi,

How are things going. Things are pretty good out here. Its warm now, only 10° below 0. We were playing pretty good, but then guys started getting hurt. Last week against Birmingham, I got into a fight. I only threw one punch, & 3 guys from our team jumped off the bench to help.

Well take care.

Wayne.

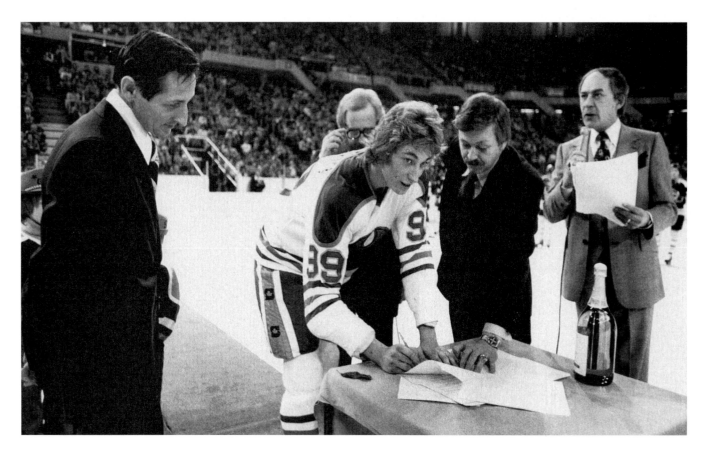

99 *Opposite top:* I celebrated my 18th birthday—January 26, 1979—with my teammates at the morning skate. Dennis Sobchuk is to my left. Joe Micheletti is right behind him. Then there's Stan Weir, Brett Callighen and Eddie Walsh, a goalie. That night I signed my new contract with the Oilers *(bottom left)*. Larry Gordon, the general manager, signed me to a 21-year deal. It would have run to 1999. The team had options, but every six years was guaranteed. My dad really encouraged me to sign the contract. They were waving around an awful lot of money and I was still improving and it made no sense not to sign it, so I was happy to sign. But, believe it or not, by signing with the Oilers I had to accept that I might never get into the NHL. Nobody knew then if Edmonton was going to get into the League, so by signing this deal I was saying, "Well, if I stay in the WHA, I'm going to be in this league forever." If the WHA would have stayed together, I might never have gotten to the NHL.

99 Early in my WHA career with the Oilers I played with Dave Semenko. He was a great teammate and very well liked by everybody in the locker room. He probably had the most inaccurate image of anyone in the game. He was known as a goon or a rockhead, but the ironic thing was he was pleasant, witty and gentle. I mean, he would never hurt anyone, and it used to always surprise us when he actually would fight. You knew he had to be mad to actually get into a fight because he was such a nice person.

Rewriting the
NHL Record Book
EDMONTON
1979 – 1988

1979-80

99 I faced off against Stan Mikita to start my first NHL game *(above)*. Brett Callighen is my left winger. There were only 9,000 people at the Chicago Stadium that night. It was still loud—the horn was crazy—but I remember thinking there's nobody here.

Welcome to the NHL! Serge Savard gives the hot-shot rookie a shove.

99 My dad took this picture at the Wayne Gretzky Centre in Brantford. He said he didn't have any good action shots, so I went over one day and did it for him.

99 In my early years I didn't use much tape on my stick. Like having no laces in my gloves, it was because of Bobby Orr. When I was a kid I always used to see Bobby Orr with no laces in his gloves and no tape on his stick. Unlike Orr, I did wear socks in my skates. I wanted to stay warm. I didn't love him that much!

99 *Opposite:* Brett Callighen and I before the Oilers' first NHL game at Maple Leaf Gardens on November 22, 1979. I loved everything about the Gardens. It was the best out-of-town building to play in. The visitor's dressing room was tiny. It stunk and was sweaty and all that kind of stuff, but it was hockey.

Gus Badali (*at right*) was my first agent. It was tough to leave him, but the thing was that he and Mike Barnett had become partners and Mike was living in Edmonton. I just felt there was a lot more convenience and that Mike and I would work more closely on everything. Gus and I are still good friends.

99 *Opposite:* I started setting up behind the net when I played junior B for the Vaughan Nationals. Because of my age difference and size difference, it became my way of survival. Back in those days, Phil Esposito could stand in the slot because he was so big and strong. If I stood there, I'd get knocked over, so that's why I started going behind the net. I actually studied hours of footage of Bobby Clarke doing it and what he did to make it successful, and that's where I learned it. Over the years I just kept working on it, and developing it, and I got more comfortable back there. I got better at it, and it became a situation where teams didn't know how to defend it.

In alone on Colorado Rockies goalie Glenn "Chico" Resch. Gretzky scored on the play.

Setting up behind Daniel Bouchard of the Atlanta Flames.

1980-81

99 Everybody tried to make a big deal out of Wilf Paiement wearing #99 in Toronto, but I couldn't see why. I mean, I had basically 140 points in my life in this league. I didn't own anything. I thought it was fine that he wore 99.

From left to right: Wilf Paiement, Darryl Sittler, Gretzky and Brett Callighen. The linesman is John D'Amico.

99 This is what would happen if I set up in front of the net instead of behind it.

Celebrating a last-minute goal against the New York Rangers. Number 4 is Ron Greschner.

99 Pat Boutette of the Hartford Whalers is looking for a fight, but Mark Messier has already grabbed him.

Gretzky dekes Capitals goaltender Al Jensen.

99 *I don't know why, but I would have to rank myself as less than average on breakaways. Especially in the early days in Edmonton. I missed more breakaways then than I did towards the end of my career. Ironically though, I scored a lot of breakaway goals in the playoffs. Overtime, too. I had one penalty shot in the playoffs and I scored. But regular seasons for some reason I missed a lot. But I scored a lot too.*

Left: March 28, 1981. Wayne celebrates with teammate Doug Hicks after tying Phil Esposito's single-season record of 152 points. Gretzky went on to score 164 points that year. His 109 assists broke Bobby Orr's single-season record of 102.

Below: Earlier in the same game. The goalie is Larry Lozinski. Mark Kirton (23) and John Barrett (2) are on defense.

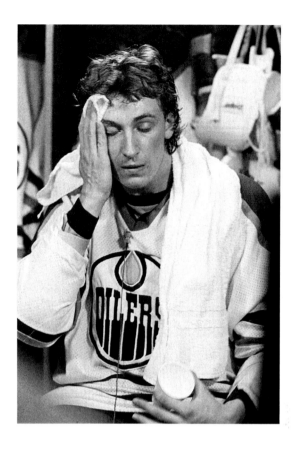

99 *Above left:* This was taken for a magazine spread about 10 great Canadians. You can't see them here, but they gave me a set of cufflinks with "99" engraved on them. This picture *(above right)* is from Hockey Night in Canada, preparing for an interview during the intermission.

99 Bill McCreary got me good during a game against the Maple Leafs. I didn't see him coming and he knocked me out cold. It was probably the hardest hit I took during my career. This is when I'm getting back up.

99 At the Forum in Los Angeles for my second All-Star Game. Our team, the Campbell Conference All-Stars, won 4–1. Our goaltender, Mike Liut, was named MVP and would also win the Pearson Trophy as the Players' Association MVP that season.

99 The playoff series against the Canadiens in 1981 was a real turning point for the Oilers. It was great to play at the Forum, but what really made it exciting for me was that Kevin Lowe and I were roommates. Playing in the Forum for him was like Maple Leaf Gardens for me. I was excited for him—and for me. Listening to Danny Gallivan and Dick Irvin. It was a great feeling.

99 The Hart Trophy *(MVP)* and my first Art Ross Trophy *(top scorer)* in 1981.

Left: This is at the 1981 Entry Draft, the day that the Oilers used the eighth pick to select Grant Fuhr. Grant would be in net for our four Stanley Cup wins.

99 My agent, Mike Barnett, organized a charity softball game in Edmonton at Commonwealth Stadium. It was wet and rainy. Luckily we got sweat pants and we had long sleeves underneath our shirts.

Below: This was a contest, I think. Mr. Big is a chocolate bar in Canada and I was their spokesman.

1981 Canada Cup

99 Me and the Flower. When I played on the Canada Cup team in 1981, I followed Guy around for six weeks. I was his shadow. Everywhere Lafleur went, I went too.

Opposite: I think I was trying to get out of the way, and ran into this elbow accidentally. Team Canada beat Sweden 4–3, then followed up with a 7–3 win over the Soviets to finish atop the round-robin standings with a mark of 4–0–1. Only a 4–4 tie with the Czechs blemished an otherwise perfect record.

Guy Lafleur, Mike Bossy and Gretzky.

99 Even though the Soviets beat us 8–1 in the final, the experience of playing at the Canada Cup was three times as good as the World Junior Championships. There was no comparison.

1981-82

99 The Penguins defensemen, Randy Carlyle and Ronnie Stackhouse, didn't want to chase me back there. The goalie is Paul Harrison, who had been recently acquired from Toronto; that's why you can see a blue plate on the back of his mask. Mark Messier and I are on the ice together, so it's probably a power-play. We're in deep, but don't be surprised if we're actually killing a penalty!

Stopped by Greg Millen of the Hartford Whalers. The defenseman is Mark Renaud.

Putting on the brakes behind the St. Louis net. Mike Liut is in goal. Rik Wilson defends.

99 Other teams didn't know how to defend against me when I set up behind the net, but my teammates became more at ease with it. As they became more comfortable, that made it more difficult for the opposing team to cover them. Jari Kurri and I would work together on it. Paul Coffey too. We made it hard for teams to defend. They didn't know exactly what to do.

99 My buddy Lyle "Sparky" Kulchisky was the trainer in Edmonton. He's been there for 25 years. He's the best. He takes care of every guy that comes through there. He stole the Stanley Cup during the 1987 finals. Slats told him to, but he stole it. Mike Keenan had this ritual. Every game he had his guys looking at the Stanley Cup, but they couldn't touch it. They could see it before game five and game six and they won both games, so before game seven he tried to get the Cup into the Flyers' locker room. Slats had Sparky put it in the back room and hide it, then they told Keenan that it accidentally went on a bus with the circus and it left town. They got the NHL security guys in a panic, and the President of the League was almost in tears, but the Cup was in the back room the whole time! When the game started and they dropped the puck they brought the Cup out and said, "Oh, we found it."

99 Trying to put everything into perspective. What's going on? Where are my guys? Where are their guys? Is Coffey coming in off the blueline?

99 I always enjoyed playing against the Sutter brothers because they were really honest. It's Brian knocking me down in this photo. They just played hard and did everything they could to win. You knew if you had your head down you were going to get cranked, but the whole time I played against them not one of them ever played illegally. They just played hard. You had to respect the way they played the game.

99 It might look like I'm going after Bob Nystrom here, but I'm not. You never questioned him. He was too tough. What's happening here is that we've had a goal disallowed and I'm not too happy about it.

50 Goals in 39 Games
December 30, 1981

99 I was on such a high the night I scored five goals to reach 50 in 39 games. But what I remember most is that I had about 10 shots in that game, and I felt like I missed four great chances, and yet I still ended up with five goals. The first one *(left)* was flukey. Charlie Huddy fired a slapshot from the point and I blasted the rebound off somebody's foot and it went in.

Second of five goals en route to 50 in 39 games, December 30, 1981.

99 With a minute left in the game, I had four goals on the night and 49 for the season. We were winning 6–5 and the Flyers pulled their goalie. I was going to do anything and everything to get to that puck. I could have outskated Paul Coffey! Bill Barber once told me a funny story that before I shot the puck he was going to throw his stick at it—and he almost did *(opposite bottom)*! With an open net, the goal would have automatically counted. It would have been a great trivia question. Who scored 50 goals without ever getting his 50th goal?

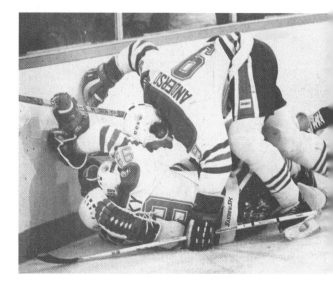

77 Goals in a Single Season
FEBRUARY 24, 1982

99 The night I broke Phil Esposito's record I didn't think I was going to get a goal at all. What I remember most about the 77th goal was that I was lucky. I stole the puck at the blueline and I got a lucky bounce. Then I was lucky again to put it between Donnie Edwards' legs. The whole bench emptied. Phil had been following us around and he was at that game. It was the biggest goal I had ever scored and then, almost before I knew it, I had added two more. I think I scored my 78th and 79th in the next two minutes. It was a great night.

Completing the hat trick with goal 79, February 24, 1982.

The NHL's first 200-point season, March 25, 1982,

99 Every time I reached a milestone with the Oilers, we'd save the puck and the trainer would mark it. Glen Sather has all my pucks from the Edmonton days locked up in a safe, except for the ones he's given to the Hockey Hall of Fame. He's told me that the rest of them are mine if I want them. They'd save and mark the milestone sticks, too. My dad has those.

99 Kirk Douglas was doing a movie in
Edmonton and he came to a game. He
was my dad's biggest hero in life, so
when I got to meet him I told him
that. My dad was more thrilled that
I met Kirk Douglas than anybody else
I ever met!

99 Anne Murray is a great lady and a
good friend. She loves sports, hockey especially. She can talk hockey
longer than I can.

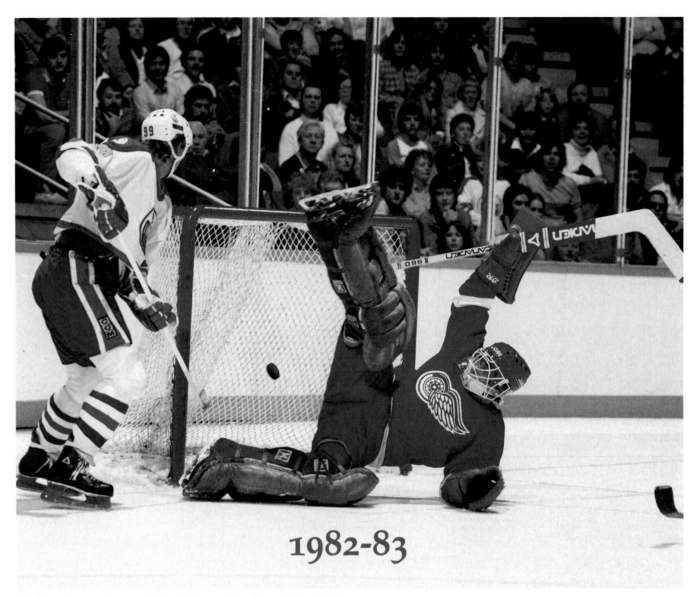

1982-83

Tucking the puck past Gilles Gilbert of the Detroit Red Wings.

99 *When I had the chance to shoot, I always looked at the top corner first. I've found that goalies, especially when they're moving from right to left, put their heads down for a split second to check their angles, automatically dropping their arms a little bit, giving me more room up high. That's what I always looked for and that's why I shot for the top corner so often.*

Looking for the top corner versus Mike Liut of the St. Louis Blues.

99 Breakaway, see that? A breakaway goal on Wayne Thomas of the Rangers. The defensemen in pursuit are (#6) Bill Baker from the 1980 U.S. Olympic team and Barry Beck (#5).

99 I always tell people that Jaroslav Pouzar *(crashing the net above)* brought the left-wing lock to the NHL. When he came over in 1982 they made a big deal out of it in Edmonton, boasting they had brought in this great, strong left winger from Czechoslovakia who was going to score 50 goals with Wayne Gretzky and Jari Kurri. The funny thing about it was that in those days with the Oilers we always forechecked the first two guys in, the third guy high. This guy came to our team, and we had no sense of where he was going to be. Plus we had a huge communication problem because of his English. It took us 40 or 50 games to realize that the reason that he was in the positions he was in was that he was playing in a Czechoslovakian left-wing lock. It took us almost a whole year to catch on to this. Once we figured it out, he was the physically strongest player I ever played with. He was also the most unselfish guy I ever played with as far as doing anything for the hockey club. He was extremely well liked by every guy. We were a young team. We were all 22, 23. Here was this 30-year-old Czech guy who came into our team and could hardly speak English. When a group of guys are together a long time they obviously develop a camaraderie, and it can form a little bit of a wall that makes it tough for other guys to feel that they're a part of the *(dressing)* room. Pouzar, however, was able to break in immediately. He was really well accepted by every guy.

Walking to practice at the Edmonton Gardens. From left: Pouzar, Tommy Roulston, Gretzky and Charlie Huddy.

99 *Opposite:* Jari Kurri and I clicked from day one. We didn't play together for the first 30 games after he joined the team in 1980–81. He played with Mattie Hagman and I was playing with Blair MacDonald because we'd had success together since the WHA. When we were put together it just clicked like nothing I've ever seen. Because he was such a great defensive player he allowed me to cheat offensively. My forte was my passing and his strength was his one-timer, so we just worked together perfectly.

99 Players keep track of their scoring streaks. Nobody wants to talk about it for fear that they'll jinx you, but quietly in the locker room, everyone talks about it behind your back. In this photo *(right)* I've just set a new record with points in 29 consecutive games. I went on to record a 51-game scoring streak in 1983-84. As the streak grew, the pressure kept increasing. I remember a game in Chicago when the streak got to 46. The Black Hawks pulled the goalie. I scored into the empty net with five seconds left and the fans were booing. The night the streak ended I was devastated, but it relieved a lot of pressure. It was a thrill to be compared with Joe DiMaggio and his hitting streak of 56 games. He came to one of the games where I set up a goal. "Explain that to me," he said. "It's an assist," he was told. "It assists a goal." "So it's not about goals?" he asked. He was told no. Then DiMaggio said, "Well, that's not really a streak."

Penalty shot stopped by Pat Riggin, November 24, 1982.

99 *Left:* Empty net goals aren't always as easy as they look. Harry Neale said I was the greatest empty net goal scorer in hockey history when I scored an empty netter against Montreal in the 1993 Stanley Cup finals.

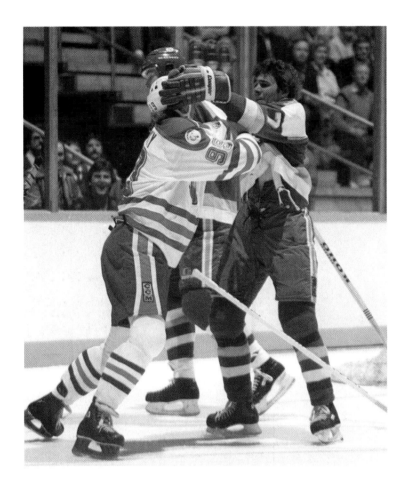

99 My fight with Neal Broten was probably the stupidest thing I ever did in my career. That night I was presented an award as Sports Illustrated's "Sportsman of the Year" and in the pre-game presentation, this guy from the magazine went on and on about how I was such a great sports-man. I think that I was in the penalty box before he got back to his seat. I don't even remember why it started, it was so silly. But Neal and I often laugh about it because nothing happened and because I don't think either one of us ever fought again.

Is the game over yet?

99 The first time I wore the "C" in Edmonton was when our captain Lee Fogolin didn't play in a Super Series game against the Soviets in 1983. The Super Series was more than just an exhibition game, and we played hard, but it certainly didn't have the drama of the Canada Cup. We won this game 4–3.

99 *Below:* That's my brother Brent in his room at my parents' house. Varadi is the street they live on. My mother had this Hotel Varadi sign because they always had so many people going in and out.

99 John Garrett had been great in goal during the first half of the 1983 All-Star Game when I scored four goals in the third period. The score had been 2–0 for us. He'd stopped Mike Bossy on a breakaway and handled a couple of tough shots from Bryan Trottier. He was phenomenal. They awarded a car to the game's MVP and he had it won. But then every time I came off the ice in the third period, John would say to me that he had lost another tire. I'd score again and he'd say, "I've lost another wheel." When I got the fourth goal he said, "You got the car." I just got a little bit lucky. And I don't know how I lost that tooth.

One-on-one against Calgary Flames defenseman Paul Reinhart.

99 *We won the Campbell Conference for the first time in Chicago. It makes me sad that players won't pick up the trophy today. I think that's wrong. They should be happy they won it. They should be proud. And obviously the superstition doesn't seem to work because the last two years both teams that didn't pick up their conference trophy lost the Stanley Cup. So my recommendation is you start picking it up. I just think it's wrong that they don't acknowledge the trophy.*

99 The amazing thing about the first Stanley Cup series against the Islanders was that we outshot them 35–24 in game one and we lost 2–0 on an empty net goal. Billy Smith basically stood on his head, shutting us out for the first time in 198 games. We were young and immature. The average age wasn't much more than 20 years old. After we lost game one, we were reeling and they got some confidence. The Islanders really taught us a good lesson that year. We admired them so much as a team. We took everything that we learned from them and it helped make us a championship team. So the loss in this series really propelled us to greater heights.

99 *Opposite:* We went to Russia in the summer of 1983 and we did a video with Vladislav Tretiak. My family and his family, basically comparing the lifestyle of the Soviet players and the lifestyle of the Canadian players. Pavel Bure was one of the kids in the video.

I played with John McEnroe *(below)* at a charity tennis tournament in Aspen, Colorado. McEnroe and I both played our best when we were feisty. Early in my career, it angered fans and other players because I was often fired up and yelling, but there's no question that I played much better hockey when I played with my emotions on my sleeve. It could pump up my team. It got all of us going.

Playing a charity golf event with Grant Fuhr. No caddies.

With Andy Warhol. His painting of Wayne hangs in Gretzky's Toronto restaurant.

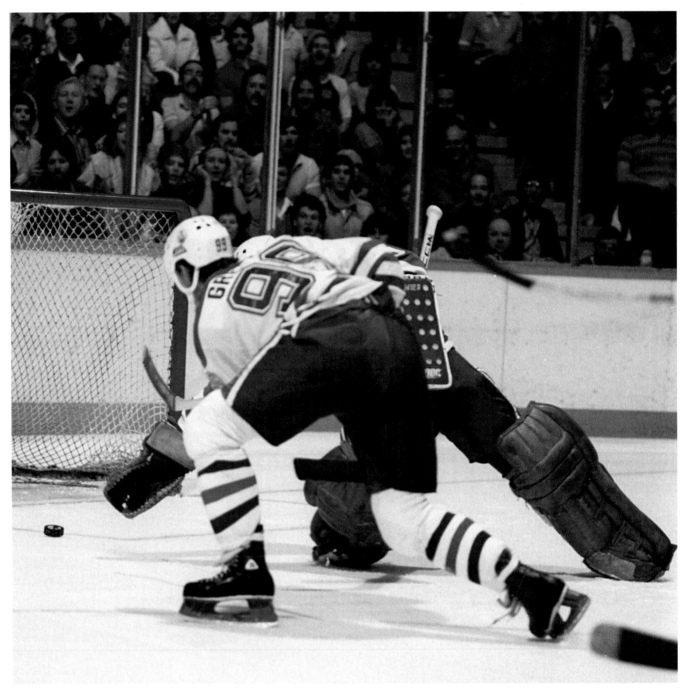

Having lost in the Stanley Cup finals the previous spring, the team dedicated itself to playing sound two-way hockey, reducing its goals against. Gretzky's league-leading point total would slip from the previous season's 212 to "only" 196, but he would set a new single-season assist record with 125.

1983-84

99 Lee Fogolin approached me to take on the captaincy before the start of the 1983-84 season. I was proud to accept his suggestion, but nothing changed within the team itself. The same respect was still held for everyone, regardless of who wore a letter on their sweater.

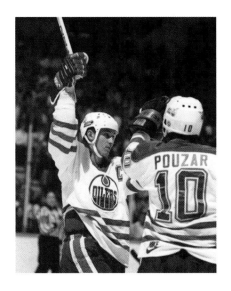

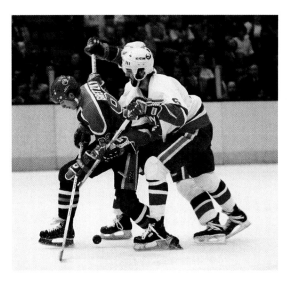

99 Riding my bike home from practice during the playoffs. People don't do that anymore. Check out my Yankees cap.

Four of the game's greats: Mark Messier, Bryan Trottier, Mike Bossy and Gretzky.

99 Everyone thought there was a huge rivalry between the Oilers and the Islanders, and obviously there was because we played so much in playoffs. But we didn't have hatred towards them. We respected how hard they worked and how unselfishly they played as a team. We've said it many times—what we learned from them propelled us to bigger heights and helped us win championships. I think that the fact that our guys wanted to win so badly, we listened and learned from everyone and that helped us win.

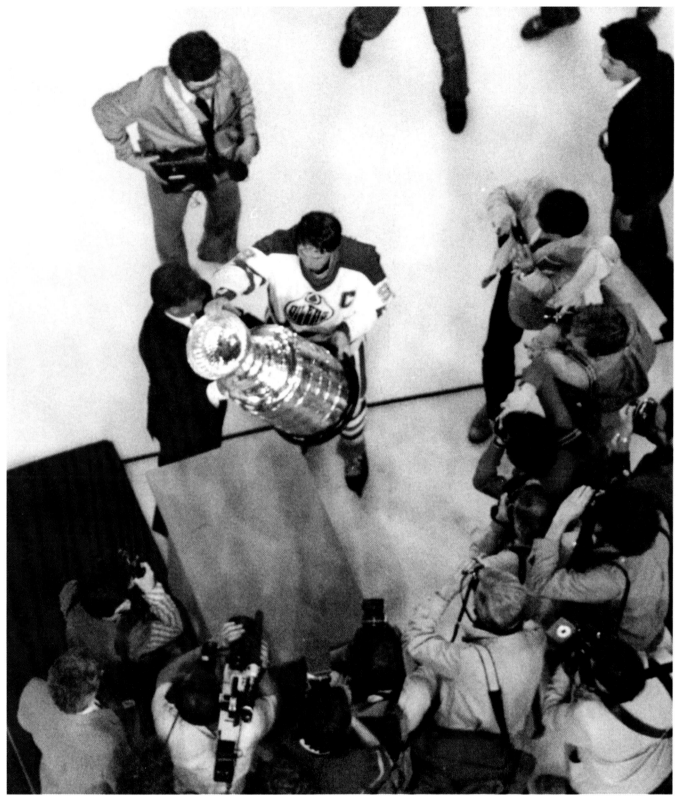

99 When we won the Stanley Cup nobody really knew what to do. Nobody within the organization, as far as coaches and players went, had ever won the Cup, so when they gave it to us and we had the Cup in the locker room I remember I said to Slats, "What do we do with the Cup?" He said, "The Cup's yours. You guys take it." So we were the first team that started taking the trophy from house to house, to restaurants, to friends, to bars, and hospitals. Glen basically said, "It's your Cup." Now the rules have changed, but in those days we just took it everywhere.

Paul Coffey with beard and Gretzky with Stanley Cup, 1984.

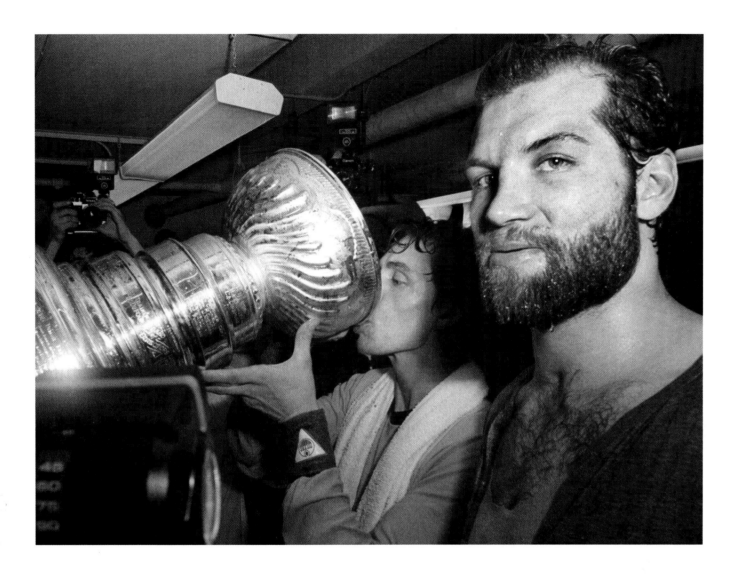

99 Dave Semenko (*above at right*) was a huge part of our success, and not only in the locker room. He played extremely well when we first won the Stanley Cup. He had come a long way as a player and he was a big contributor.

Andy Moog (*right*) doesn't seem to get the credit that he deserves. He was a great goaltender.

99 From the top: me, Patty Hughes, Dave Lumley, Dave Semenko and Rick Chartraw.

99 Joey Moss. Big Joey. He's worked in the Oiler locker room for 20 years now. They've been really good to him. This photo was taken at a charity golf tournament we used to have for the mentally handicapped. Joey still works in the Oiler locker room.

1984 Canada Cup

Left: with Mike Bossy at Canada Cup training camp.

99 Later in my career, I did turn down a couple of offers to go to Europe for the World Championships, but I never turned down the Canada Cup. I played in all of them. We almost missed the playoffs in 1984. We had to beat the Czechs just to get in. Then we beat the Soviets in overtime and swept Sweden in the best-of-three final.

Low snap-shot from just inside the faceoff circle against the New Jersey Devils, January 25, 1985.

Celebrating a goal against the Detroit Red Wings.

99 *Right:* This was taken at a charity event in the Northlands Coliseum. It would be an open practice, and then they'd have us play a team of 10-year-olds. I went in net.

Covered by Andre Savard of the Quebec Nordiques.

99 Greg Millen. I scored a lot on Millsey. *(21 goals in all. Only Richard Brodeur [29] and Mike Liut [23] were victimized by Gretzky more often.)*

99 This was Esa Tikkanen's first game, because he's wearing number 14 instead of his regular number 10. Slats put him in for game two against the Flyers. I said, "Who is this guy?" and Slats says, "You better get to know him, because he's your left winger." We won that game 4-1. He was my left winger, but I couldn't understand him. That's why I'm talking to Jari. He thought that Tik spoke English, but he didn't speak any. So that's why we're huddled. I felt like Joe Montana calling a play. I'm telling Jari and Jari's telling Tik. He's telling Jari back, and then Jari's basically saying to me, "Don't worry about it, Gretz. He doesn't know what you're saying."

Fending off Philadelphia's Ron Sutter.

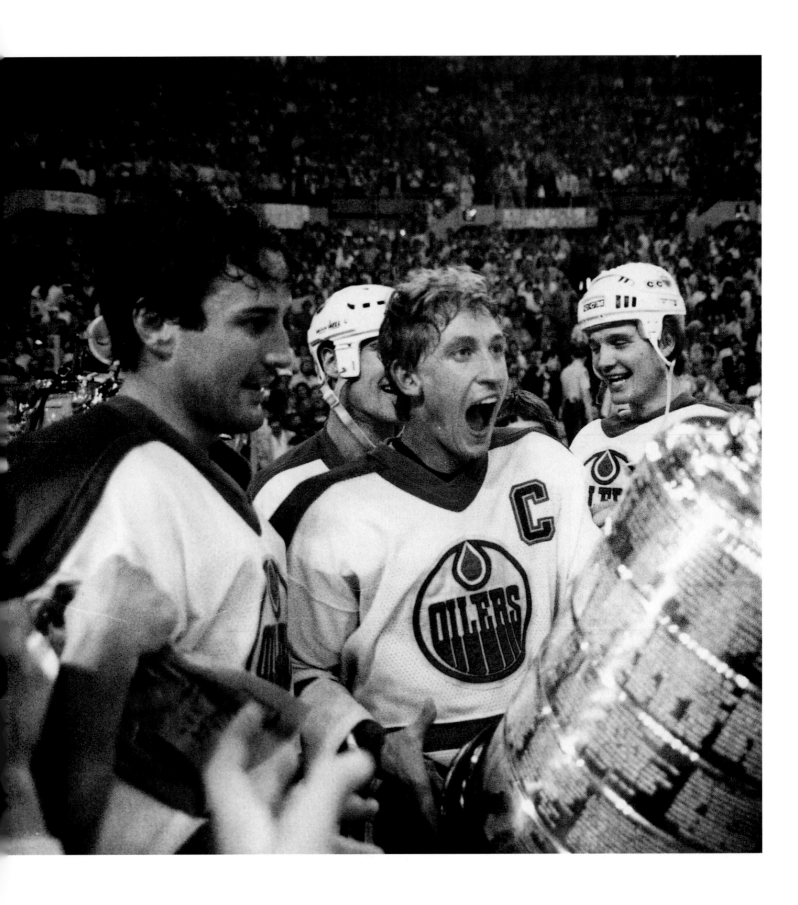

99 *At this point in my career, when we beat Philadelphia for the Stanley Cup in 1985, I was playing as well as I ever played. We beat the Flyers in five games. The whole team was terrific. Paul Coffey and Jari Kurri and I were really clicking as a unit. We were so strong skating and passing that after this season the NHL changed the four-on-four rule for penalties.*

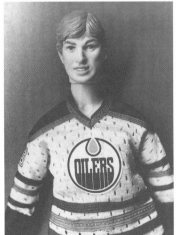

Above: Keith Gretzky checks out his hometown's efforts to honor his brother.

Above left: The family rec room. Brent takes on Glen in table hockey, while Keith keeps tabs on Mork, the family cat. Some of Wayne's Hart Trophy plaques can be seen on the wall.

Left: The Wayne Gretzky doll.

1985-86

99 *Above:* Ten Oilers in the 1986 All-Star Game. That was a huge controversy because Slats picked the team. In those days the coach added a couple of guys. But we definitely deserved to have that many guys there because we were romping through the league. Everyone was mad that we had 10 guys there, but there's not really one guy that didn't deserve to be there.

Left: They had Brantford Day before an Oiler game, and my brother Brent came out.

In close on the Rangers' John Vanbiesbrouck.

99 One of the first times we played against each other I said to Mario Lemieux, "You come into the league and you're the young guy like I was. You're playing against guys like Guy Lafleur, and Marcel Dionne, and Mike Bossy, and Bryan Trottier. Then before you know it you're the older guy and the young guy is coming after you." I remember telling him that, and I remember exactly how I felt being 18 years old the first time I went into the Forum playing against Lafleur, and how my mind felt when I played against Bobby Clarke in the Spectrum. You just got excited. The first time Mario and I played against each other I said, "I've still got that same excitement. I'm gonna be ready to play against you." Because I knew he was a great player and I wanted to play well.

Eluding the Islanders' Stefan Persson for a shot on goal.

Tripped up by Calgary's Gary Suter, above, and Steve Bozek, right.

99 In all the years I played, the rivalry between Calgary and Edmonton was the best. The rivalry between the Islanders and the Rangers is close, but unfortunately over the three years that I played in New York, we didn't have teams that were at the same level I experienced with Calgary and Edmonton. When both teams have an opportunity to win a championship, the rivalry becomes intense. I'm sure it was the same way when the Islanders and the Rangers were both Stanley Cup contenders, but in my time the best rivalry I was a part of was Edmonton versus Calgary.

99 We had one game where we lost to Calgary 9–2, and it was a brawl. One of our guys was in a fight in front of our bench, and Tim Hunter popped him. His nose — you heard it go "splat." And the guy on our team, Kevin McClelland, looked to the bench and said, "Didn't feel a thing." He kept fighting. Tim Hunter, who was still standing in front of our bench, said, "That guy is crazy."

99 Losing to Calgary in the 1986 playoffs was devastating for everyone. Especially with the way the goal was scored. *(Rookie defenseman Steve Smith put the puck in his own net.)* I remember that after that game I got dressed, and I talked to the media, and I left the locker room. Not abruptly, but I didn't hang around and sulk either. I remember saying, "Hey, sometimes you gotta deal with bumps in the road. We lost and we're all devastated that we lost, but we're healthy, and we gotta start planning today—right now—that we're gonna come back and win next year." And that's what we did. All of us as a team did that. We bounced right back.

99 We always had a ball at the NHL's postseason awards ceremonies. It was a kind of reward for all the days of hard work. And you know Glen was innovative in the sense that he liked to be around the guys. There was no talk of, "Well, he's the coach, we can't sit down and have a beer with him."

1986 Oiler award winners from left: Gretzky, MVP and top scorer;
Glen Sather, coach of the year; and Paul Coffey, top defenseman.

Glenn Anderson was #9 to Gretzky's #99 for 591 games in Edmonton.

1986-87

99 Glenn Anderson was always a big-game, big-goal player. Although at times he was overshadowed by several of the other big names on the Oilers, he was never underrated by Oilers management or by his teammates themselves.

99 I never played against Bobby Orr, so Denis Potvin was
the best defenseman I played against. No question.
Potvin played hard. He was smart, strong and fast. And
he was mean if he wanted to be mean. Early in my
career, Potvin used to play with Gordie Lane, and I used
to think, "Oh my God." I was 19 years old and I had
those two guys to go out against.

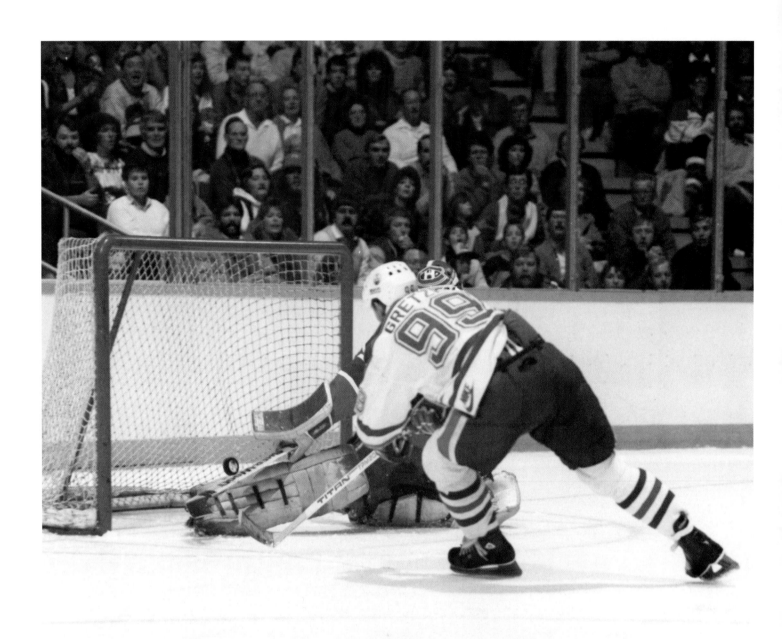

Gretzky scores on Patrick Roy of the Montreal Canadiens, November 8, 1986.

99 *Opposite:* The 500th goal was exciting because when I was growing up, there was only Gordie Howe and Maurice Richard and a few others with 500 goals. That was a benchmark for success in professional hockey. When I got my 500th, that was one of my first big milestones that dealt with longevity, not just single-season performance. Usually guys holding up their 500th-goal puck are kind of battle scarred and nicked up, but I was fast!

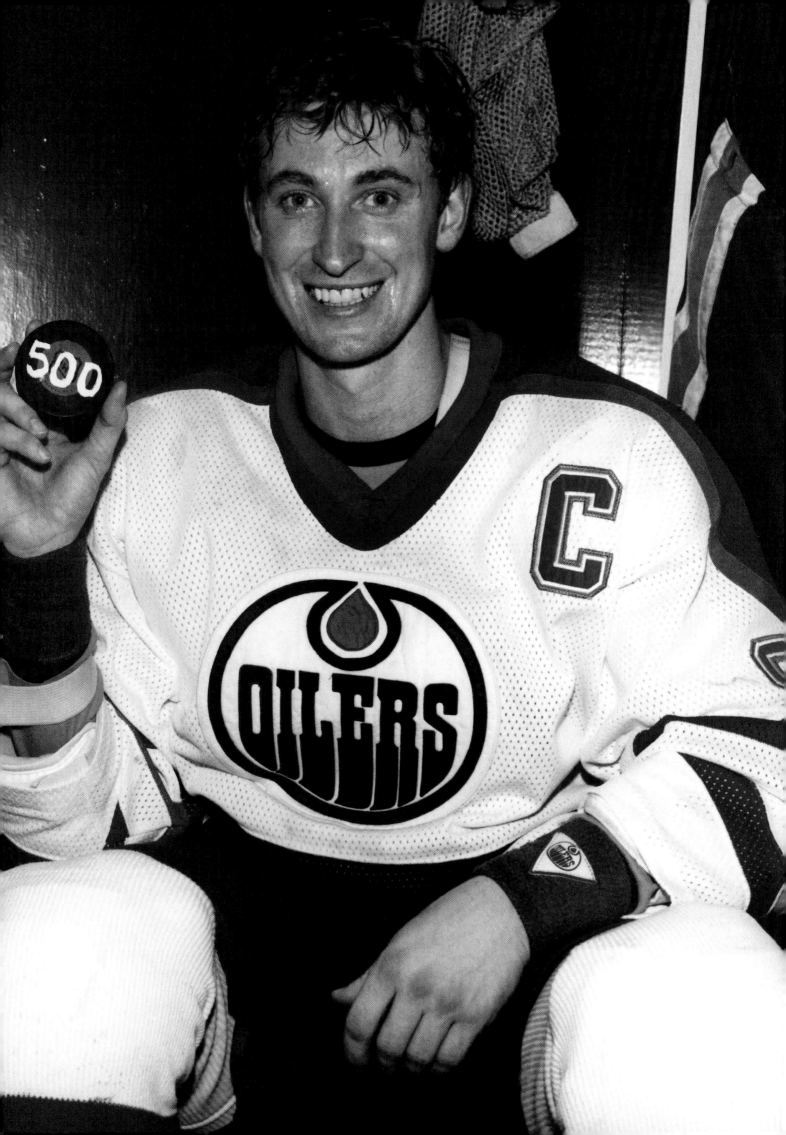

With Mario Lemieux, Rendez-Vous 87.

Rendez-Vous 87

99 Rendez-Vous 87 was a two-game series with the Soviets that replaced that year's All-Star Game. Both games were played in the Colisée in Quebec. We switched sweaters at the end. I'm wearing Viacheslav Fetisov's in this photo *(right)*. Rendez-Vous was one of the first times my wife Janet saw me play. I won a car as the most valuable player on the NHL team. A year later, she asked me why I had won the car when the best player on the ice was a Russian (Valeri Kamensky) and he had only won a stereo. I told her, "Well, he lives in the wrong country."

99 Paul Coffey added so much to my arsenal. As a defenseman, he'd feed me pinpoint long passes. He was one of the fastest and smoothest skaters in the history of hockey, so he could make a pass from his own end to start a play and then join the rush late looking for a passout. He had a great shot, so he could finish what he often started.

Facing off against
Detroit's Steve Yzerman.

99 Dale Hawerchuk was one of the most under-rated players I ever played against. As a matter of fact, Winnipeg was probably the best team in the league that could never beat the Oilers in big games. *(General manager)* John Ferguson always built good clubs there. They were big and they could skate, but unfortunately for them, the Oilers were always one step better. I thought the biggest difference was that we had Grant Fuhr in goal. Hawerchuk was an excellent player, but unfortunately for the Jets, they played in an era when they had to get past us to advance in the playoffs.

Enjoying a freak snow storm that hit Edmonton between games one and two of the 1987 Stanley Cup finals.

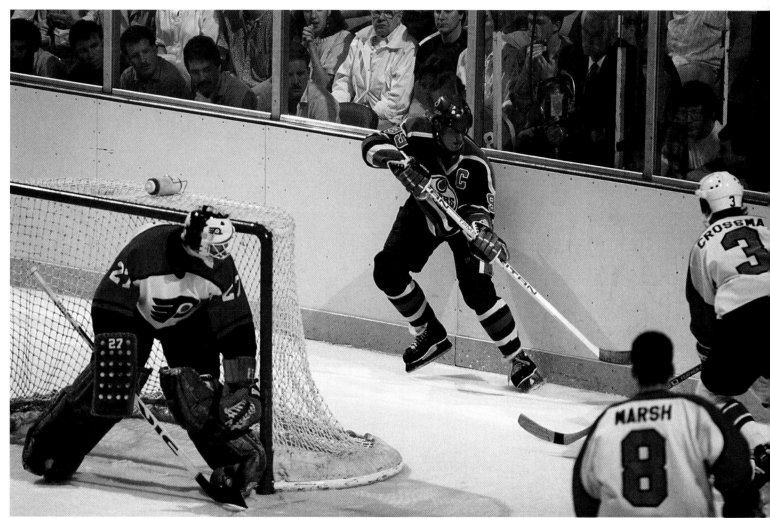

Goalie Ron Hextall watches Gretzky over his shoulder as Doug Crossman and Brad Marsh close in.

99 *When we won again in 1987, everyone on the team except Steve Smith kind of collectively knew that I was going to pass the Stanley Cup to him. There was no question that what had happened the year before was devastating to him and his family, but it wasn't his fault we lost the Stanley Cup and that's the way our guys looked at it. It was just one of those things. And he went on to help win three more Stanley Cups. He became a huge part of that team's core.*

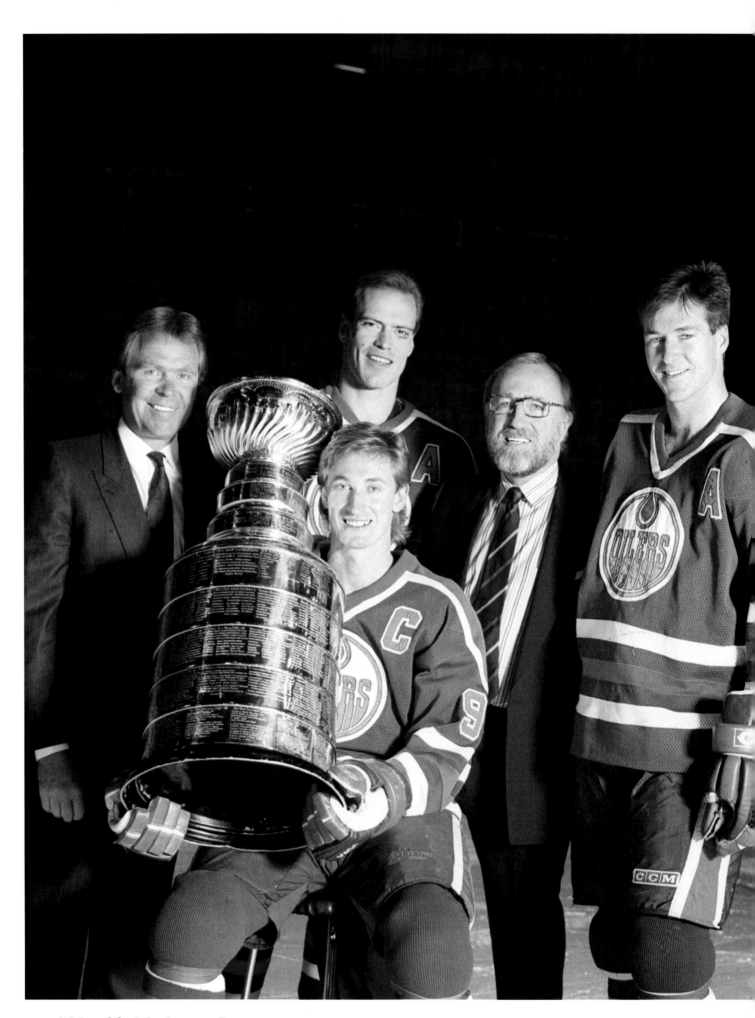

Above: 1987 NHL awards; Art Ross Trophy (scoring), Campbell Bowl, Pearson Award (Players' Association MVP), Stanley Cup, Hart Trophy (MVP). Opposite, left to right: Sather, Gretzky, Messier, Pocklington, Lowe.

99 I liked Peter Pocklington *(opposite, second from right)*. Peter and I had a really good relationship, and we still do. Peter would come into the locker room and he'd want to bet me. He'd say, "OK, you get three goals today, I'll buy you a new pair of shoes. If you don't then you owe me five autographed sticks." He always tried to get the guys excited. He would come into the locker room and say, "If you guys win this game today, or win the championship, I'll give you two tickets to Hawaii." He always treated the players well, and the players always liked him. After he'd been around, every guy felt like he was on top of the world.

1987 Canada Cup

99 Game two of the 1987 Canada Cup final (*above*) was probably my best international game. We beat the Soviets 6–5 in overtime. Mario had three goals and I had five assists and we played really well together. I always gauge my games on the basis of the level of competition that we have, and I felt that that particular Soviet team was one of the game's greatest. Our team was very good too, so the competition between the two teams was extremely high, and the pressure was intense. I felt that I was able to raise my level of play.

Celebrating after setting up Mario Lemieux for the Canada Cup-winning goal. Lemieux scored with 1:26 remaining to give Team Canada a 6–5 win over the Soviets in the third and deciding game of the tournament final.

99 There's been a lot of talk that I taught Mario how to compete at the 1987 Canada Cup, but to be honest with you I don't think I taught him anything. I do think he watched guys like Coffey and Messier and myself. There were a lot of Oilers on that team in '87, and he was still a young guy. There's so much pressure placed upon a guy at 24, 25 years old in this game. I think Mario really enjoyed himself on that team and fit in well with all the guys. He sat back and watched guys who had won championships, whether it was me or Paul or Kevin Lowe or Messier. And there's no question that that tournament and that experience helped make him a better player.

Gretzky played against two of his brothers in the NHL. Keith, above, faced Wayne in an exhibition game for Buffalo prior to the start of the 1987-88 season. Brent, inset, who played 13 games for the Tampa Bay Lightning, lined up against his brother in 1993-94.

1987-88

99 It was a proud moment for my dad to see that the dream of playing in the NHL had come true for three of his sons. Unfortunately during the time Brent was playing with Tampa, my dad suffered a serious injury to his head that diminished his awareness of the significance of the event.

Room with a view. The offensive zone, as seen from Gretzky's office.

Jari Kurri played more games with Gretzky (858) and assisted on more goals by #99 (196) than any other teammate.

1,050 Assists

MARCH 1, 1988

99 It was exciting to break Gordie Howe's assist record. I remember the guys teasing me and saying, "You've got a long way to go *(to break Howe's goal-scoring record)."* In fact, it took six years.

He shoots, he …

99 This was my last goal as an Oiler, against Boston in game four-and-a-half of the 1988 finals. *(The Oilers swept the Bruins in 1988, but one game was suspended due to a power failure in Boston Garden.)*

Opposite bottom: Optional workout during the 1988 finals. I think I was on the ice telling somebody to look at Slats who was down there trying to teach somebody how to score goals.

99 I knew that this was going to be my last year in Edmonton. I had too many friends who were telling me that Peter (*Pocklington*) had been calling around trying to sell me. By the time we hoisted the Cup, I figured that I wasn't going to be an Oiler much longer so I rallied the troops together for a picture on the ice.

99 That's Janet and me in the locker room. My last Oiler Cup was the only one she was around for.

99 It was an amazing wedding. The nicest one I've ever been to. I think everyone had a great time.

99 I knew the day the trade was announced was going to be a tough one. We flew to Edmonton, and I spent the whole time trying to figure out a way to stay away from Glen *(Sather)*. I knew that he was going to try to talk me out of it, but by that time I was so disappointed that Peter *(Pocklington)* had tried to sell me that I had made my mind up that it was time to move on. When I got there Glen spent a good hour and a half working on me. He wanted to kill the trade right there, but I just knew in my heart that it was the right time to move along. We ended up going forward and we made the transition happen. Obviously that hour and a half in Edmonton was devastating, not only for me, but for my family, and for my friends. I left not only fans and teammates, but a ton of friends I had spent a lot of time with up there.

"The Trade"
AUGUST 9, 1988

Speaking to the media beside Oilers owner Peter Pocklington at the trade day press conference in Edmonton.

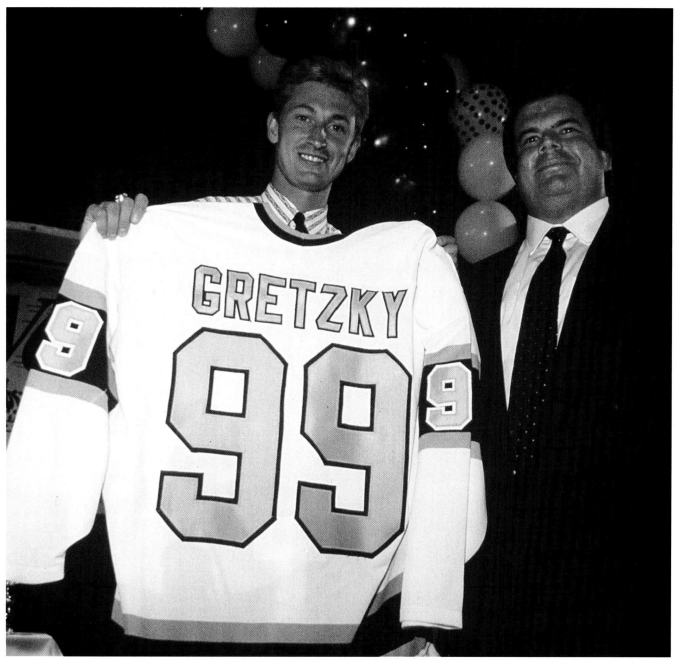

With Kings owner Bruce McNall on the day of the trade.

99 *After the emotion of the press conference in Edmonton, flying to Los Angeles was very different. When we landed in California, there were balloons and whistles and everyone was excited. So we went from an intense low to an amazing high all within four hours.*

The King of Kings
Los Angeles
1988 – 1996

First training camp as a King in Victoria, B.C, September 1988.

99 I remember beginning training camp with the Kings in Victoria, B.C. *(above)* and it hit me about the second day I was there. I called Kevin Lowe and I remember saying, "I don't know what I've done here." Because I'd gone from the Edmonton Oilers, who won four Cups in five years, and were maybe one of the greatest teams ever, to this team that was 19th out of 21 teams. You didn't have to be an Einstein to figure out the talent level had dropped. I remember being a little bit shaken up as to what my situation was. Then, at the first exhibition game in L.A., I remember Bruce McNall being so mad because there were only about 12,000 people at the game. So I told him, "You've got to be patient. We have to build this thing. Rome wasn't built in a day."

Stepping onto the ice for the first time as a King in the Great Western Forum, 1988-89 preseason.

99 Esa Tikkanen *(right)* and I were good friends when we played together and now we were arch-rivals against each other. I knew he wanted to win and I understood that. We both played very emotionally out there and sometimes it got carried away.

Left: 1989, last of nine Hart Trophy wins in the decade.

Below: Gretzky's Kings eliminated his former club, the Oilers, in seven games in the first round of the 1989 Stanley Cup playoffs.

With Jay Leno on the Tonight Show.
Hockey had become a hip night
out in Los Angeles.

99 Lorne Michaels called me to do "Saturday Night Live" *(below)* but I said no, I can't act.
The next thing I know, I'm flying to New York on some other business and I read in
USA Today that Wayne Gretzky will be hosting "Saturday Night Live." I thought there
must be some mistake, but my wife said "I called them back and said you'll do it. This is
something you're going to treasure for the rest of your life." I remember being so mad,
but it was the greatest thing I ever did. I had so much fun. It was so enjoyable. Everyone
was so nice. It was one of the greatest weeks that I've ever had in my life. People seem to
remember the Waikiki Hockey sketch where I was the busboy. Well, you get to pick what
you want to do and that was one that I didn't want. But Lorne said, "If you do this,
you're gonna put this show over the top. If you don't do it, everybody's just going to
say, 'Ah, it was OK.'" And I said, "Alright." And that's how he talked me into it.

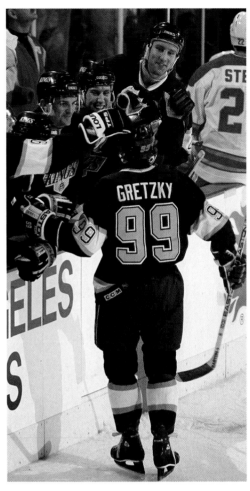

Neutral site game in Phoenix vs. Calgary.

99 We had a plan *(to promote hockey in the United States)* when I went to L.A. I said to Bruce *(McNall)*, "You know the way you sell the game is not by giving away cars and promotional things. What we need to do is hit the grass roots. We need to get kids wanting to play hockey and be hockey players, because when that happens they're going to tell their parents they want to go watch NHL hockey games. So the Kings really worked hard, starting youth hockey programs in Los Angeles and the surrounding areas. They started working hard at getting more and more kids involved. And every-where we went as a hockey team every player on the team was always available and accessible, as I think all the guys are in the NHL. Of course, timing has a little bit to do with everything. The NHL's biggest stars were exciting offensive players at that time. And then the first "Mighty Ducks" movie came out, which really helped hockey. So I think it was just a culmination of a lot of things that helped sell the game.

99 I wore this flag all year (1991) on my helmet, because my American cousin Kenny fought in the Gulf War. You can't see it in this photo, but on the other side of the helmet, I had printed his initials.

99 I'd get really excited during games, and if I thought that something didn't go the way I wanted it to go—or something didn't happen the way I wanted it to happen—I'd get terribly upset. There's no question that sometimes I'd lash out. Early in my career, reporters would write that I was a whiner, but I knew how far to push referees, how far I could take them and the effect it would have on my teammates. As adamant as I got, a lot of times I'd be yelling and screaming and I'd be saying, "How's your wife and family?" Everyone thought I was screaming and hollering at the referee.

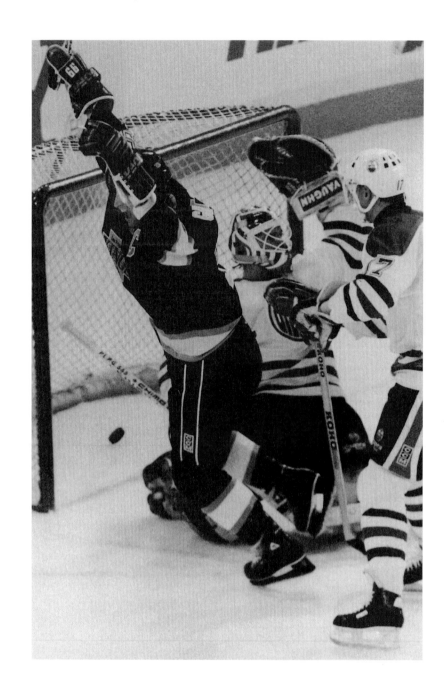

99 Because we had beaten them in the playoffs the year before, the rivalry between Los Angeles and Edmonton became huge. Of course, the people in the stands wanted me to break Gordie Howe's record there, but they were hoping the Oilers would win 5–3 and I'd get a point. Instead, it was 4–3 Edmonton and there was about a minute to go. One of our guys kept the puck in and shot it in front of the net. It went off Dave Taylor's foot and came right to me. For some reason I was wide open and I just backhanded it in. Beacause I had admired Gordie for so long, this mark was important to me. It was a big point to get.

1,851 Points
OCTOBER 15, 1989

Wayne and Janet hosted charity tennis and softball events.

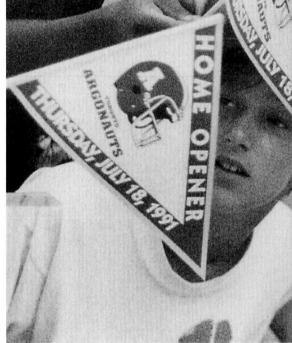

Gretzky joined Bruce McNall and John Candy as a co-owner of the Toronto Argonauts of the Canadian Football League.

1991 Canada Cup

99 Although this particular test was for the 1991 Canada Cup, we used to do fitness testing every year. The funny thing about these tests is that when I was younger I didn't really care about them. I knew I was in shape. I went to camp, and whatever I scored *(on the test)*, I scored. As I grew older, it became a personal challenge for me to be able to score better than I did the year before and to be able to compete with all the young guys. The test became a great measuring stick for me as I got older in my career, and I really took a lot of pride in it. And it was tough.

99 The 1991 Canada Cup was the only time I played for Team Canada in Maple Leaf Gardens. We opened the tournament there against Finland with a 2-2 tie. Mike Keenan was our coach and he went nuts in practice the next day. He threw his stick into the stands, but no one in the media noticed it.

99 After the tie with Finland, we picked it up. We beat the USA in Hamilton and then came back to Toronto to play Sweden *(above and left)*. This was one of my best games for Team Canada, a 4-1 win. I had three assists in the first period, two of which were on shorthanded goals. We controlled the game from there.

We beat the Americans two straight in the finals. I wasn't in uniform when the trophy was presented *(opposite)* because I injured my back on a hard hit by Gary Suter in game one of the final.

Wayne and Walter Gretzky mural, Gretzky's Restaurant, Toronto.

99 *Left:* This picture was taken when my restaurant opened in Toronto. That's Vladislav Tretiak on the left and my dad beside me. The other man is Bill Cornish, Sr. whose family I lived with when I moved to Toronto in 1975.

99 This is one of the first times my son Ty went skating. We're at our practice rink with the Kings. I cut down the stick in the locker room. I didn't realize it was autographed till after we got out there.

99 *In my estimation this was the best game I ever played in the NHL because it was game seven, it was on the road and it felt like the L.A. Kings versus Canada, not just the Maple Leafs. I don't think anybody expected us to win, but we did. 5–4. I had three goals and an assist. I've said it many times, but I think that was the best game I played in the NHL.*

Game Seven, Campbell Conference Final

MAY 29, 1993

99 Throughout the 1993 playoffs, Doug Gilmour (*#93*)
was playing as well as I've ever seen him play.

99 I wanted that trophy *(the Clarence Campbell Bowl)* all the time. It's magnificent. To me, the high point of the entire history of the Los Angeles Kings is that we won the trophy and went on to the 1993 Stanley Cup finals.

After defeating Toronto, it was on to Montreal to face the Canadiens in the 1993 Stanley Cup finals.

99 Game one against Montreal in the Stanley Cup finals was our second game in a row on the road in the playoffs. We had won game seven against Toronto, then we won game one 4-1. Then we went into game two and it was our third straight game on the road. It was like a road trip and we're in the Stanley Cup finals. We were a little tired to be honest with you, and you know it was a misfortune for us that they checked Marty McSorley's stick. They could have checked any one of about seven guys. Unfortunately for Marty he was the guy that got caught with the illegal curve. Did it cost us the Stanley Cup? I don't know, but there's no question there was a huge swing in the momentum of the series. They went on to win three games in overtime after that. People always ask me about it, and I always say if it wasn't for Marty we would never have got to the finals. I'm sure it's a mistake that's going to haunt all of us for a long time, but I don't think it's the sole reason why we lost the Stanley Cup.

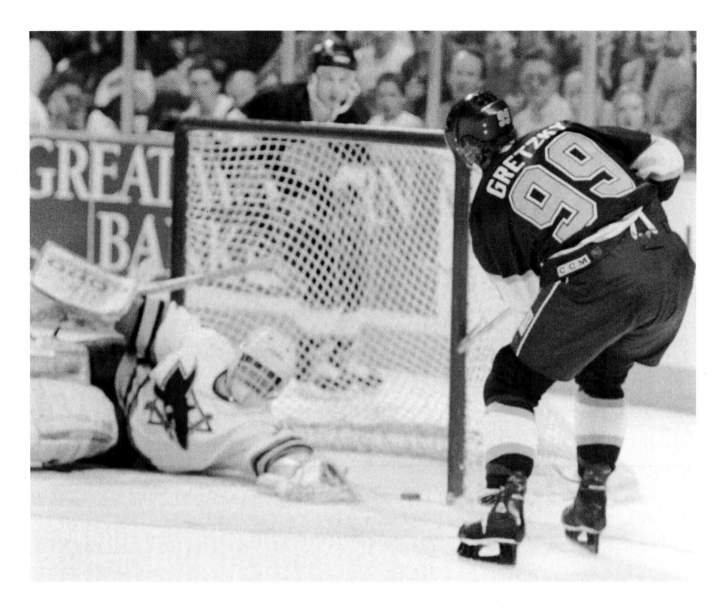

99 Goal number 801 *(above)* came in the last minute of the game. I think it tied the score 6–6. I had the empty net and Arturs Irbe made the save, but then I got the rebound and poked it in to tie the record. Before I went into the game where I scored #802, I remember my wife saying to me, "You know this is going to be one of the highlights of your life. Make sure that you really sit back and enjoy it. Savor the moment." She's a sports fan like I am, and when you watch athletics you love to see people enjoy when they excel and do something very special. A lot of times when it happens to you, you forget the moment. Before you know it, it's over. So when I scored my 802nd, it was one of the first records that I really thought about and took everything in, enjoying the moment. I will never forget that goal because I took the time to enjoy it immensely.

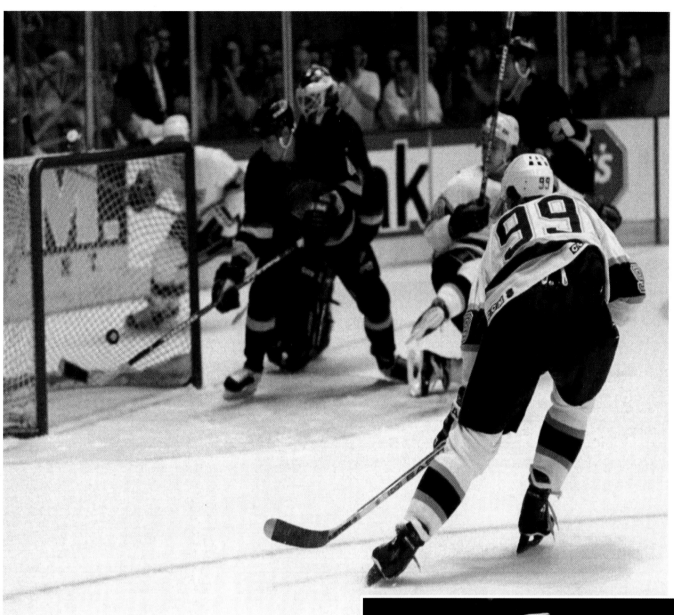

802 NHL Goals

MARCH 23, 1994

The NHL presented Gretzky with a commemorative book made up of scoresheets from every game in which he scored.

The Ninety-Nine Tour came about because we were locked out by the NHL and couldn't play hockey at the beginning of the 1994-95 season, so a few of us put together a team that would go over to Europe and play some games. I got Mark Messier and Jari Kurri to play for our team, and Grant Fuhr and Al MacInnis. We made a few phone calls and before we knew it we had sold out about seven arenas in Europe. We chartered a plane so everybody could take one person, and a lot of the single guys took their fathers. We had some fun. It turned out to be one of the greatest road trips in hockey history.

Gretzky and agent Mike Barnett in Stockholm's Globen Arena at the start of the Ninety-Nine Tour.

99 Rick Tocchet, *left,* is one of the most respected players in the game today. Each year, you can count on him both to score 30 to 35 goals and to be as tough as anyone in the league. I've always admired his work ethic.

Keeping an eye on Kevin Miller of the San Jose Sharks. Note the alternate Kings jersey.

Briefly Blue

ST. LOUIS

1996

St. Louis got the Great One on February 27, 1996.

99 *Opposite:* This was my first goal with the Blues. One of the reasons I went to St. Louis was to play with Brett Hull. Brett and I are good friends and we enjoyed playing together. He's one of the great players to ever play our game. It's a shame that neither one of us is still playing in that city. It's too bad for the hockey fans of St. Louis. I really thought when I got traded to St. Louis that I was going to finish my career there. The people there were good to me, but basically I ended up leaving St. Louis because the Blues never really offered me a contract.

The World Cup of Hockey played in September 1996 allowed top NHL players to compete for their national teams in a competition similar to the Canada Cup. Gretzky, in his sixth major international event, again captained Team Canada and played strongly, finishing with seven points in six games. Team USA, behind the red-hot goaltending of World Cup MVP Mike Richter, defeated Canada in the tournament final.

World Cup of Hockey, 1996

99 I was always excited to play for Canada. I had great memories from Canada Cup tournaments I'd played in, so I looked forward to the World Cup, thinking that it would be my last time in a Team Canada uniform. *(It wasn't. Gretzky would also play in the 1998 Winter Olympics in Nagano, Japan.)* Unfortunately we didn't get the result that we wanted in the World Cup, though we could have just as easily won the event. Despite losing the final, we had great fun playing together again.

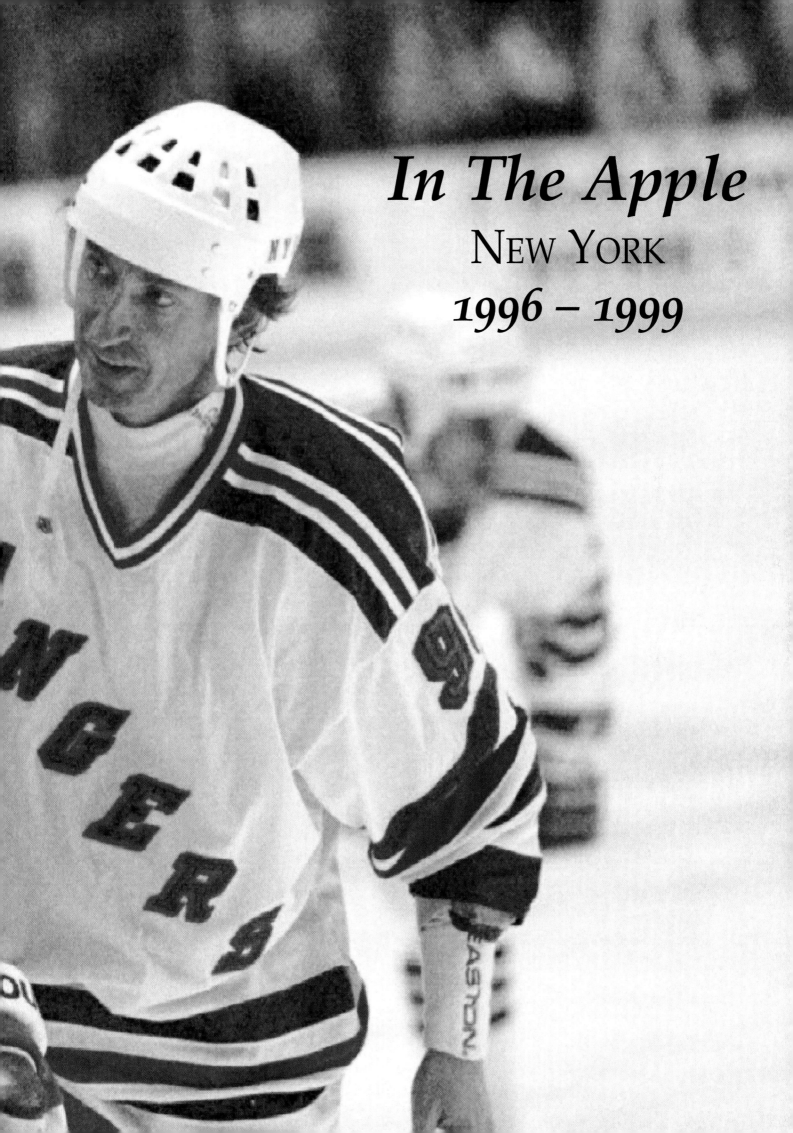

In The Apple
NEW YORK
1996 – 1999

Above: Gretzky signs a contract extension with Rangers general manager Neil Smith.

99 *Above:* This is my signing in New York. That's Ty, looking thrilled to be there. New York is a unique place because they love winners and they want their teams to win. They are the biggest fans in the sense of winning and losing. If you lose, they die with your losses and they can be critical, but there's no better place in the world to win.

99 This was my first picture in a Ranger uniform. It was actually taken in Los Angeles at Iceoplex, the Kings' practice rink. They sent the uniform out with a photographer because they needed pictures once the signing was announced.

99 *People were ecstatic that Mark (Messier) and I were back together, especially in New York. Both of us always loved the Letterman show, so we had a riot doing it together. We never thought, when we were 19-year-old teammates, that one of us would ever appear on the show, let alone the two of us together.*

99 Trainers and equipment managers always made my life easier, setting everything up for me, ready to go. Their help is an extremely underappreciated part of a hockey player's routine. Trainers also take care of players' kids and my boys visited the locker room frequently. In this photo, my son Ty is with Rangers equipment managers Mike Folga and Cass Marques.

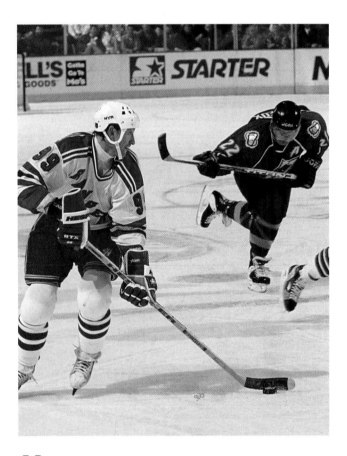

99 Two of my friends in hockey: Colorado's Claude Lemieux, *left*, and Kevin Stevens, *right*. Claude's family and mine have become close over the last few years. His personality off the ice is the exact opposite of what you see on it. He will do anything to win during a game, but away from hockey he is a gentleman. Kevin is a rare kind of player. Of all the teammates I've had, he is the one who was most liked by everyone on the club. Everyone in the locker room enjoys his company.

99 ways to do business: (top left) the Wayne
Gretzky Collection of menswear is sold at
The Bay stores across Canada; (top right)
Wayne Gretzky's Roller Hockey Centers
are located in the Western U.S.; and (left)
terrazzo floors and pressed tin ceilings
frame sports memorabilia in the bar
at Wayne Gretzky's Restaurant in
downtown Toronto.

Celebrating a playoff hat trick against the Florida Panthers, April 23, 1997.

99 Even though we didn't win during my first year in New York, our playoff run in 1997—where we got to the semifinals before losing to the Flyers—was a highlight of my career and lots of fun. The whole experience confirmed to me that New York is an amazing place to be an athlete. New Yorkers expect their teams to win, but if an athlete plays his heart out and the fans know it, they will rally around him and give him the benefit of the doubt every single day.

Winter Olympics, 1998

99 I was really nervous getting off the train in Nagano. It was one of the only times I ever got nervous in a crowd because I was trying to communicate with people who didn't understand what I was saying. After that, we had a great time in the Olympic Village. The Canadian team had a common room where everyone would congregate every night, whether it was the skiers or the curlers. We developed a camaraderie with our teammates from other sports. I think that a lot of the athletes expected the hockey players would think they were bigger or better than other people, but that wasn't the case at all. We had more fun in there than anybody, and I think the other athletes really enjoyed that about us. The Village was one of the great parts of the whole experience for me.

99 The Olympics were one of the greatest highlights of my career. Not because we were having an opportunity to play for a gold medal but because of the fact that I got a chance to play for Canada in the Olympic Games. I was so proud to be part of Canada's team, that when Bobby Clarke called me and told me that I was not going to be the captain I told him I'd be the water boy if they wanted. I think the NHL has to stay in the Olympics, especially with the next Games being in the United States. There's the fact that a lot of Canadians can go down to see the games, plus there's the opportunity for prime time TV as well. I think it's to the benefit of the NHL to go back to the Olympic Games.

99 *I would absolutely have liked to have been given a chance in the shootout against the Czechs in the Olympic semifinals. I think that the only mistake Team Canada made in Nagano was not that I didn't take a shot, but that instead of choosing our best breakaway scorers, we seemed to select our shooters based on how well they had done against (Czech goalie Dominik) Hasek in the Skills Competition at the NHL All-Star Game.*

Back on Broadway.

99 Hockey Night in Canada play-by-play man Bob Cole, *below*, is one of the nicest people in hockey. We get along so well because we both love the game. I really enjoy being in his company.

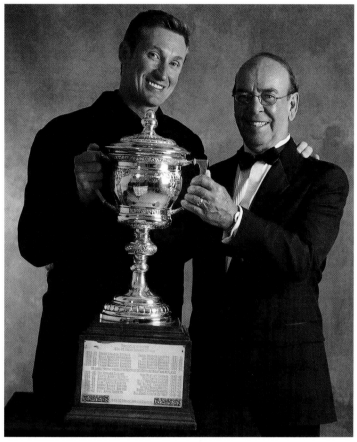

With Bob Cole and the Lady Byng Trophy. Gretzky won this award for gentlemanly conduct on five occasions including 1979-80, his first NHL season, and 1998-99, his last.

99 I played my last game at Maple Leaf Gardens on Saturday, December 19, 1998. The Leafs were scheduled to move out the following February, so we knew that this was our last chance to play in the old barn. It was a special day that started right from the morning skate, when we wore our full game uniforms and had an on-ice team picture taken *(left)*. We walked around the arena in the morning and all the players savored the time. After the game was over that night, I just sat on the bench for an extra 30 seconds or so. I didn't want to move because I knew then that I'd played my last game there. To me, the Gardens remains one of the greatest buildings in all of sports.

99 The last goal of my career (*above*) made 1,072 in the NHL and WHA, regular season and playoffs combined. One more than Gordie Howe. About a month before I scored it I had hurt my back. During my last trip through Calgary and Edmonton, everybody had wanted me to score the goal then, but my back was so sore I couldn't move my arm. I played the two games, but when we came back I went into the hospital. I was about to announce the next day that I would be out indefinitely. That night Gordie Howe called me and said, "I'm going to China and I wanted to congratulate you on breaking the record before, because I won't get a chance to." And I said, "Gordie, tomorrow morning I'm announcing that I'm out indefinitely. You could be back in a few weeks and we could still be tied." And he said, "Oh you'll be back playing. You'll get it done. Don't worry about it." I remember hanging up the phone and saying to my wife, "You know, I really don't know if I've got a chance to break this record now." Well fortunately my rehabilitation went well and I got an opportunity to come back. But now what was disappointing for me was that every single game that we played my teammates tried everything they could to get me a goal, and I couldn't get one. When this goal finally went in I was more thrilled to take the pressure off those guys than for any goal I ever scored.

1,072 NHL and WHA Goals

MARCH 29, 1999

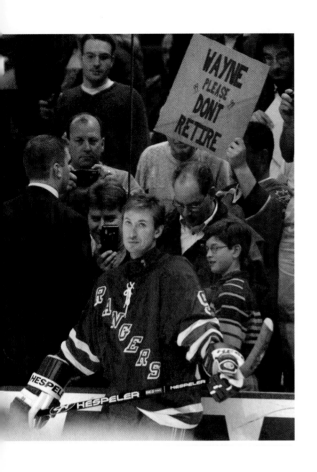

99 Jean Chretien, Canada's Prime Minister, called me on the day of my last game in Canada, which was in Ottawa, and invited me for tea with the Premier of China. I hated turning down the Prime Minister, but I told him I couldn't make it because I had a game to play. As for the game, a friend of mine happened to be in New York and he flew my family in his plane to Ottawa. Otherwise they wouldn't have been there. Then things just kind of unfolded, starting with the reception I received from the crowd during the warmup, and ending with the way they treated me after the game ended. (*Gretzky was named all three stars.*) When I came into the locker room and the crowd was still applauding, all the guys said, "You gotta go back out there." So I went out again and when I came back in and saw my teammates, that's when I got emotional. What made the Ottawa night so special was that none of it had been planned. It was a night I'll never forget.

99 With John Muckler at my last practice. John is a really astute man, and he lives and dies the game of hockey. He has made a lifetime study of the game and was probably able to teach me better than anybody I've ever had the chance to know, coaching me in both Edmonton and New York. When I decided to retire, one of the hardest conversations was the one I had with John. He told me he'd really like to have me back and tried to talk me out of retiring, but didn't try too hard, which was nice. He was like a parent to me. He is one of the great people you get to be around in this game, and I'm glad I got a chance to play for him.

Final Game
APRIL 18, 1999

99 My final game was an emotional time. It was great that my friend Mark Messier was there. He's a beloved athlete in the city of New York, and I'm happy that he came back. Mario showed up and that was a nice surprise. I remember the warmup a blur of people and signs. We lost to the Penguins in overtime and I recorded my final assist on a goal by Brian Leetch. I'll always be moved by my memories of what it felt like in Madison Square Garden at the end of the game.

NHL Commissioner Gary Bettman announced the retirement of #99 throughout the NHL before the game. From left to right: Bettman, John Davidson, Mario Lemieux, Glen Sather, Mark Messier, Gretzky, Brian Leetch, Jeff Beukeboom.

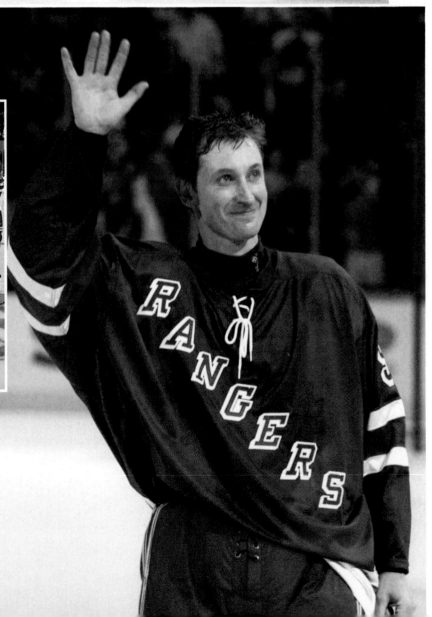

Below: Young hockey players in Edmonton responded to Gretzky's retirement by gathering at his statue outside the Oilers' home rink.

99 *When it was all over I didn't want to take my uniform off. I kept it on for about an hour and a half, the longest I had ever worn it after a game. I knew that when I took it off, it would be for the last time, so I just took my time. But when I finally did hang up my skates and take off my sweater that final time, only one thing went through my mind: I'm sorry it's over, but I know I made the right decision.*

Photo Credits

Acknowledgements

Wayne Ayer; Michael Barnett, IMG Hockey; Anne-Marie Beaton, Canadian Press; Francine Bellefeuille, The Globe and Mail; Tom Bitove, Wayne Gretzky's Restaurant; Paul Bontje; Jean Bradshaw, Toronto Star; Rob Bundy; Craig Campbell, Hockey Hall of Fame; Mike Carroll; Anita Cechowski, NHL Images; Copywell, College Street, Toronto; Bill Cornish; Caron Court, Edmonton Journal; Design Infinity; Al Fox, Wayne Gretzky's Restaurant; Andrea Gordon, Canadian Press; Darrell Holowaychuk, Edmonton Oilers; Heather Jessop; Lynda Keith, Hudson's Bay Company; Steve Knowles, Edmonton Oilers; Anton Leo; Jacquie Mah; Perry Mah; David McConnachie, NHL; Andy McGowan, NHL Images; Gord Mills, The Pro Lab Inc.; NHL Public Relations Department; Karen Polbmer, The Sault Star; Theresa Regnier, D.B. Weldon Library, University of Western Ontario, John Rosasco, New York Rangers; Murray Simkin, Wayne Gretzky's Roller Hockey Centers; Bill Tuele, Edmonton Oilers; Tommy Turner, Hudson's Bay Company, Peter Wilton.

Animation cel courtesy of Hersh Borenstein, Frozen Pond, Toronto 1 800 461-0965.

Bruce Bennett Studios: i, ii-iii, 2, 3, 13, 18 left, 47 top, 49, 50-51, 55 bottom, 59, 80, 87, 92, 96 top, 99 bottom, 103 bottom right, 106, 118, 119, 123, 124 top, 132, 137 top, 140 bottom, 150, 153, 154 top, 155, 158 bottom, 159, 160 top, 167 bottom, 168, 171-173, 175 top left, top right, bottom right, 180, 184 top, 187 bottom, 188, 189, 192, 193, 197, 198, 203, 205, 206, 213, 214 top, 216, 217, 220 inset, 222 inset, 225;

Andrew D. Bernstein: 139, 141 bottom, 163, 164-165, 167 top, 170 top, 183, 187 top;

Denis Brodeur: 65, 66 bottom, 136, 137 bottom, 199 bottom;

Ken Dorse: 40 top, 41;

Doug Bundy: 31 bottom, 32 top and upper inset;

Cornish Family Collection: 20-21, 35, 36, 39, 47 bottom, 52 top, 57 bottom, 160 bottom, 182 bottom;

CP Picture Archive: iv, vi, 24 bottom, 25 bottom, 32 bottom, 33, 63 left, 83 bottom, 95 bottom, 100, 112 inset, 113, 122 top, 133, 148 inset, 186, 196 bottom; *(Charles Rex Arbogast* 202 top, 220 top and bottom, 222 top; *(Doug Ball)* 43; *(Gordon Beck)* 48 top; *(Dean Bicknell)* 78 top; *(Dave Buston)* 9, 56, 74, 105, 130 bottom, 138, 154 bottom; *(Mary Butkus)* 196 top; *(Paul Chaisson)* xiii, 212, 219 top; *(Fred Chartrand)* 69 top; *(Bob Deoppers)* 46; *(Hans Deryk)* 82 bottom, 210 bottom; *(Kevork Djansezian)* 211; *(Eric Draper)* 191; *(Blaise Edwards)* 147; *(Bruce Edwards)* 78 bottom; *(John Felstead)* 145; *(Dennis Floss)* 82 top; *(Ron Frehm)* 200-201, 208 bottom; *(Brian Gavriloff)* 83 top; *(Courtesy Globe and Mail)* 91 right; *(Bill Grimshaw)* 69 bottom, 120; *(Bruce Harper)* 101 left; *(Jonathan Hayward)* 18 right; *(Ed Kaiser)* 152; *(Doug Kanter)* 202 bottom; *(Rusty Kennedy)* 209; *(Bill Kostroun)* 208 top; *(Larry MacDougal)* 129; *(John Mahoney)* 45; *(Keith McNichol)* 79 bottom; *(Jim Morris)* 88; *(Jacques Nadeau)* 52 bottom; *(Ken Orr)* 48; *(Charlie Palmer)* xiv, 115 bottom; *(Mike Pinder)* 89 top; *(Susan Ragan)* 17, 169 bottom, 190; *(Stuart Ramson)* 19; *(Reed Saxon)* 169 top; *(Doug Shanks)* 135; *(Alan Singer)* 204; *(Greg Southam)* 175; *(Chuck Stoody)* 68 top, 166; *(Ray Stubblebine)* 96 bottom; *(Mario Suriani)* 101 bottom left; *(Walter Tychnowicz)* 222 bottom; *(Nick Ut* 73; *(Van Horne)* 148; *(Kathy Willens)* 210 top; *(Paul Wodehouse)* 98, 141 top; *(Larry Wong)* 151.;

Edmonton Journal (Rob Galbraith) 162; *(Brian Gavriloff)* 109 bottom, 121; *(Ed Kaiser)* 157; *(Mike Pinder)* 108, 142; *(Steve Simon)* 161;

Edmonton Oilers Collection: xi, 4, 6, 10, 57, 58, 60 top, 61, 63 right and bottom, 64 top, 67 top, 70-72, 75, 84-86, 89 bottom, 90, 91 top left and bottom, 93, 97, 94 top, 99 top, 101 top, 102, 103 top and bottom right, 104, 107, 109 top, 111, 114, 115 top, 116, 117, 125-128, 130 top, 134, 140 top, 143, 144, 149, 158 top,;

The Globe and Mail: 34 bottom; *(Hans Deryk)* 146; *(Jack Dobson)* 31 top; *(Harry McLorinen)* 30; *(John McNeill)* 60; *(Dennis Robinson)* 23, 25 top, 29, 122 bottom;

Gretzky Family Collection: viii, x, 24 top, 26, 27 bottom, 28, 53, 81, 112 top, 124 bottom;

Wayne Gretzky's Restaurant: 207 bottom;

Wayne Gretzky's Roller Hockey Centers: 207 top right;

Hockey Hall of Fame (Gretzky Collection): 22, 27 top, 34 top, 37, 38 bottom, 42, 131; *(Doug MacLellan):* v, 185 bottom; *(Miles Nadal):* 66 top;

Bill Livingstone: xii;

London Free Press Collection, The D.B. Weldon Library, University of Western Ontario: 32 lower inset, 62 top, 122 inset;

Doug MacLellan: 194-195, 214 inset;

NHL Images: 44, 64, 66 bottom, 219 top; *(Dick Loek)* 67 bottom; *(Sylvia Pecota)* 215; *(Diane Sobolewski)* 218;

Reuters Archive Photos (Mike Blake) 156; *(Gary Hershorn)* 175 bottom left, 221;

Craig Samuel: 207 top left, background photo;

The Sault Star: 38 bottom, 40 bottom;

The Toronto Star: 54, 55 top, 62 bottom, 76, 77, 95, 110, 170 bottom, 176-179, 181, 182 bottom; *The Toronto Star (K. Faught* 185 top; *(Doug Griffin)* 79 top; *(C. McConnell):* 184 bottom;

The Toronto Sun: (Stan Behal) 207 top left; *(Warren Toda)* 214 bottom.

NHL Records Held or Shared by Wayne Gretzky

Wayne Gretzky holds or shares 61 records listed in the *NHL Official Guide and Record Book*: 40 for the regular season, 15 for the Stanley Cup playoffs and six for the All-Star Game.

REGULAR-SEASON RECORDS (40)

GOALS (6)

MOST GOALS: 894 (1,487 games). Second: 801 — Gordie Howe, 26 seasons, 1,767 games

MOST GOALS, INCLUDING PLAYOFFS: 1,016 — 894 regular season and 122 playoff. Second: 869 – Gordie Howe, 801 regular season and 68 playoff

MOST GOALS, ONE SEASON: 92 – 1981-82, 80-game schedule. Second: 87 – Wayne Gretzky, 1983-84, 80-game schedule

MOST GOALS, ONE SEASON, INCLUDING PLAYOFFS: 100 – 1983-84, 87 goals in 74 regular season games and 13 goals in 19 playoff games. Second (tied): three players

MOST GOALS, 50 GAMES FROM START OF SEASON: 61 – 1981-82 (Oct. 7, 1981 to Jan. 22, 1982, 80-game schedule); 1983-84 (Oct. 5, 1983 to Jan. 25,1984, 80-game schedule. Next (third): 54 – Mario Lemieux, 1988-89 (Oct. 7, 1988 – Jan. 31, 1989, 80-game schedule)

MOST GOALS, ONE PERIOD: 4 – (Tied with 10 other players) Feb. 18, 1981, at Edmonton, third period (Edmonton 9, St. Louis 2)

ASSISTS (6)

MOST ASSISTS: 1,963 (1,487 games). Second: 1,102 – Paul Coffey, 19 seasons, 1,320 games

MOST ASSISTS, INCLUDING PLAYOFFS: 2,223 – 1,963 regular season and 260 playoff. Second: 1,226 – Paul Coffey, 1,090 regular season and 136 playoff

MOST ASSISTS, ONE SEASON: 163 – 1985-86, 80-game schedule. Next (eighth): 114 – Mario Lemieux and Wayne Gretzky tied, 1988-89, 80-game schedule

MOST ASSISTS, ONE SEASON, INCLUDING PLAYOFFS: 174 – 1985-86, 163 assists in 80 regular season games and 11 assists in 10 playoff games. Next (tied for 11th): 121 – Mario Lemieux 1988-89; 114 assists in 76 regular season games and seven assists in 11 playoff games

MOST ASSISTS, ONE GAME: 7 – (tied with Billy Taylor) done three times – Feb. 15, 1980 at Edmonton (Edmonton 8, Washington 2); Dec. 11, 1985 at Chicago (Edmonton 12, Chicago 9); Feb. 14, 1986 at Edmonton (Edmonton 8, Quebec 2). Second: 6 – 23 players

MOST ASSISTS, ONE ROAD GAME: 7 (tied with Billy Taylor) – Dec. 11, 1985 at Chicago (Edmonton 12, Chicago 9). Second: 6 – four players

POINTS (4)

MOST POINTS: 2,857 –1,487 games (894 goals, 1,963 assists). Second: 1,850 Gordie Howe, 1,767 games (801 goals, 1,049 assists)

MOST POINTS, INCLUDING PLAYOFFS: 3,239 – 2,857 regular season and 382 playoff. Second: 2,010 – Gordie Howe, 1,850 regular season and 160 playoff

MOST POINTS, ONE SEASON: 215 – 1985-86, 80-game schedule. Next (fifth): 199 – Mario Lemieux, 1988-89, 80-game schedule

MOST POINTS, ONE SEASON, INCLUDING PLAYOFFS: 255 – 1984-85; 208 points in 80 regular-season games and 47 points in 18 playoff games. Next (sixth): 218 – Mario Lemieux, 1988-89; 199 points in 76 regular-season games and 19 points in 11 playoff games

OVERTIME SCORING (1)

MOST OVERTIME ASSISTS, CAREER: 15. Second: 13 – Doug Gilmour, 16 seasons

SCORING BY A CENTER (6)

MOST GOALS BY A CENTER, CAREER: 894. Second: 731 – Marcel Dionne, 18 seasons

MOST GOALS BY A CENTER, ONE SEASON: 92 – 1981-82, 80-game schedule. Next (third): 85 – Mario Lemieux, 1988-89, 80-game schedule

MOST ASSISTS BY A CENTER, CAREER: 1,963. Second: 1,040 – Marcel Dionne, 18 seasons

MOST ASSISTS BY A CENTER, ONE SEASON: 163 – 1985-86, 80-game schedule. Next: Gretzky holds first through fifth positions

MOST POINTS BY A CENTER, CAREER: 2,857. Second: 1,771 – Marcel Dionne, 18 seasons

MOST POINTS BY A CENTER, ONE SEASON: 215 – 1985-86, 80-game schedule. Next (fifth): 199 – Mario Lemieux, 1988-89, 80-game schedule

SCORING BY A ROOKIE (1)

MOST ASSISTS, ONE GAME, BY A PLAYER IN HIS FIRST NHL SEASON: 7 – Feb. 15, 1980, at Edmonton (Edmonton 8, Washington 2). Second: 6 – Gary Suter, April 4, 1986 at Calgary (Calgary 9, Edmonton 3)

PER-GAME SCORING AVERAGES (4)

HIGHEST GOALS-PER-GAME AVERAGE, ONE SEASON: 1.18 – 1983-84, 87 goals in 74 games. Second (tied): 1.15 – Mario Lemieux (1992-93, 69 goals in 60 games) and Wayne Gretzky (1981-82, 92 goals in 80 games)

HIGHEST ASSISTS-PER-GAME AVERAGE, CAREER (300 MIN.): 1.321 – 1,963 assists in 1,487 games. Second: 1.183 – Mario Lemieux, 881 assists in 745 games

HIGHEST ASSISTS-PER-GAME AVERAGE, ONE SEASON: 2.04 – 1985-86, 163 assists in 80 games. Next (eighth): 1.52 – Mario Lemieux, 1992-93, 91 assists in 60 games

HIGHEST POINTS-PER-GAME AVERAGE, ONE SEASON (AMONG PLAYERS WITH 50-OR-MORE POINTS): 2.77 – 1983-84, 205 points in 74 games. Next (third): 2.67 – Mario Lemieux, 1992-93, 160 points in 60 games

SCORING PLATEAUS (12)

MOST 40-OR-MORE GOAL SEASONS: 12 in 20 seasons. Second: 10 – Marcel Dionne in 18 seasons

MOST CONSECUTIVE 40-OR-MORE GOAL SEASONS: 12 – 1979-80 to 1990-91. Second: 9 – Mike Bossy, 1977-78 to 1985-86

MOST 50-OR-MORE GOAL SEASONS: 9 (tied with Mike Bossy) – Gretzky in 20 seasons and Bossy in 10 seasons. Second: 6 – Guy Lafleur in 17 seasons

MOST 60-OR-MORE GOAL SEASONS: 5 (tied with Mike Bossy) – Gretzky in 20 seasons and Mike Bossy in 10 seasons. Second: 4 – Phil Esposito in 18 seasons

MOST CONSECUTIVE 60-OR-MORE GOAL SEASONS: 4 – 1981-82 to 1984-85. Second: 3 – Mike Bossy, 1980-81 to 1982-83

MOST 100-OR-MORE POINT SEASONS: 15. Second: 10 – Mario Lemieux in 12 seasons

MOST CONSECUTIVE 100-OR-MORE POINT SEASONS: 13 – 1979-80 to 1991-92. Second: 6 – six players

MOST THREE-OR-MORE GOAL GAMES, CAREER: 50 – 37 three-goal games; nine four-goal games; four five-goal games. Second: 39 – Mike Bossy in 10 seasons (30 three-goal games, nine four-goal games)

MOST THREE-GOAL GAMES, ONE SEASON: 10 (done twice) – 1981-82 (six three-goal games; three four-goal games; one five-goal game) and 1983-84 (six three-goal games, four four-goal games). Next (third): 9 – Mike Bossy (1980-81, six three-goal games, three four-goal games) and Mario Lemieux (seven three-goal games, one four-goal game, one five-goal game)

LONGEST CONSECUTIVE ASSIST-SCORING STREAK: 23 games – 1990-91, 48 assists. Second: 18 – Adam Oates, 1992-93, 28 assists

LONGEST CONSECUTIVE POINT-SCORING STREAK: 51 Games – 1983-84 (Oct. 5, 1983 to Jan. 28, 1984, 61 goals, 92 assists for 153 points). Second: 46 – Mario Lemieux, 1989-90 (39 goals, 64 assists)

LONGEST CONSECUTIVE POINT-SCORING STREAK FROM START OF SEASON: 51 – 1983-84; 61 goals, 92 assists for 153 points (Oct. 5, 1983 to Jan. 28, 1984)

PLAYOFF POINTS (4)

MOST POINTS, CAREER: 382 – 122 goals and 260 assists. Second: 295 – Mark Messier, 109 goals and 186 assists

MOST POINTS, ONE PLAYOFF YEAR: 47 – 1985 (17 goals and 30 assists in 18 games). Next: 44 – Mario Lemieux, 1991 (16 goals, 28 assists in 23 games)

MOST POINTS IN FINAL SERIES: 13 – 1988 three goals and 10 assists (four games plus suspended game vs. Boston, three goals). Second: 12 – four players

MOST POINTS, ONE PLAYOFF PERIOD: 4 – (tied with nine other players) April 12, 1987 at Los Angeles, third period, one goal, three assists (Edmonton 6, Los Angeles 3)

PLAYOFF SHORTHANDED GOALS (2)

MOST SHORTHANDED GOALS, ONE PLAYOFF YEAR: 3 – (tied with five other players) 1983 (two vs. Winnipeg in Division Semifinals, won by Edmonton, 3-0; one vs. Calgary in Division Finals, won by Edmonton 4-1)

MOST SHORTHANDED GOALS, ONE PLAYOFF GAME: 2 – (tied with eight other players) April 6, 1983 at Edmonton (Edmonton 6, Winnipeg 3)

PLAYOFF GAME-WINNING GOALS (1)

MOST GAME-WINNING GOALS IN PLAYOFFS, CAREER: 24. Second: 19 – Claude Lemieux

PLAYOFF THREE-OR-MORE GOAL GAMES (1)

MOST THREE-OR-MORE GOAL GAMES: 10 (eight three-goal games, two four-goal games). Second (tied): 7 – Maurice Richard (four three-goal games, two four-goal games, one five-goal game) and Jari Kurri (six three-goal games, one four-goal game)

NHL ALL-STAR GAME RECORDS (6)

NHL ALL-STAR GAME GOALS (3)

MOST ALL-STAR GAME GOALS: 13 (in 18 games played). Second: 11 – Mario Lemieux (in eight games played)

MOST ALL-STAR GAME GOALS, ONE GAME: 4 (tied with three players) –1983 Campbell Conference

MOST ALL-STAR GAME GOALS, ONE PERIOD: 4 – 1983 Campbell Conference, third period

NHL ALL-STAR GAME ASSISTS (1)

MOST ALL-STAR GAME ASSISTS, CAREER: 12 – (tied with four players). Second: 10 – Paul Coffey (in 14 games played)

NHL ALL-STAR GAME POINTS (2)

MOST ALL-STAR GAME POINTS, CAREER: 25 – (13 goals, 12 assists in 18 games). Second: 22 – Mario Lemieux (11 goals, nine assists in eight games played)

MOST ALL-STAR GAME POINTS, ONE PERIOD: 4 – (tied with Mike Gartner and Adam Oates) 1983 Campbell Conference, third period (four goals)

PLAYOFF RECORDS (15)

PLAYOFF GOALS AND ASSISTS (7)

MOST PLAYOFF GOALS, CAREER: 122. Second: 109 – Mark Messier

MOST ASSISTS IN PLAYOFFS, CAREER: 260. Second: 186 – Mark Messier

MOST ASSISTS, ONE PLAYOFF YEAR: 31 – 1988 (19 games). Next (fourth): 28 – Mario Lemieux, 1991 (23 games)

MOST ASSISTS IN ONE SERIES (OTHER THAN FINAL): 14 – (tied with Rick Middleton) 1985 Conference Finals (six games vs. Chicago). Second: 13 – Doug Gilmour, 1994 Conference Semifinals (seven games vs. San Jose) and Wayne Gretzky, 1987 Division Semifinal (five games vs. Los Angeles)

MOST ASSISTS IN FINAL SERIES: 10 – 1988 (four games, plus suspended game vs. Boston). Second: 9 – three players

MOST ASSISTS, ONE PLAYOFF GAME: 6 – (tied with Mikko Leinonen) April 9, 1987 at Edmonton (Edmonton 13, Los Angeles 3). Next: 5 – 11 players

MOST ASSISTS, ONE PLAYOFF PERIOD: 3 — Three assists by one player in one period of a playoff game has been recorded on 70 occasions. Gretzky has had three assists in one period five times. (Ray Bourque, three times; Toe Blake, Jean Beliveau, Doug Harvey and Bobby Orr, twice)

Wayne Gretzky's Season-by-Season Career Statistics

WAYNE DOUGLAS "THE GREAT ONE" GRETZKY (GREHTS-KEE)

Center. Shoots left. 6' 185 lbs. Born, Brantford, Ontario, January 26, 1961

Season	Club	League	GP	G	A	Pts	PIM	GP	G	A	PTS	PIM
1967-68	Brantford Nadrofsky Steelers	OMHA	....	1	....	....	....	....	....	....	....	....
1968-69	Brantford Nadrofsky Steelers	OMHA	....	27	....	....	....	....	....	....	....	....
1969-70	Brantford Nadrofsky Steelers	OMHA	62	104	63	167	....	....	....	....	....	....
1970-71	Brantford Nadrofsky Steelers	OMHA	76	196	120	316	....	....	....	....	....	....
1971-72	Brantford Nadrofsky Steelers	OMHA	85	378	139	517	....	....	....	....	....	....
1972-73	Brantford Turkstra Lumber	OMHA	....	105	....	....	....	....	....	....	....	....
1973-74	Brantford Turkstra Lumber	OMHA	....	192	....	....	....	....	....	....	....	....
1974-75	Brantford Charcon Chargers	OMHA	....	90	....	....	....	....	....	....	....	....
1975-76	Vaughan Nationals	OHA Jr. B	28	27	33	60	7	....	....	....	....	....
1976-77	Seneca Nationals	OHA Jr. B	32	36	36	72	35	23	40	35	75	....
	Peterborough Petes	OHA Jr. A	3	0	3	3	0	....	....	....	....	....
1977-78	Sault Ste. Marie Greyhounds	OHA Jr. A	64	70	112	182	14	13	6	20	26	0
	Team Canada	World-Jr.	8	8	9	17	2	....	....	....	....	....
1978-79	Indianapolis Racers	WHA	8	3	3	6	0	....	....	....	....	....
	Edmonton Oilers	WHA	72	43	61	104	19	13	*10	10	*20	2
1979-80	**Edmonton Oilers**	**NHL**	**79**	**51**	***86**	***137**	**21**	**3**	**2**	**1**	**3**	**0**
1980-81	**Edmonton Oilers**	**NHL**	**80**	**55**	***109**	***164**	**28**	**9**	**7**	**14**	**21**	**4**
1981-82	Team Canada	Can-Cup	7	5	7	12	2	....	....	....	....	....
	Edmonton Oilers	**NHL**	**80**	***92**	***120**	***212**	**26**	**5**	**5**	**7**	**12**	**8**
	Team Canada	WEC-A	10	6	8	*14	0	....	....	....	....	....
1982-83	**Edmonton Oilers**	**NHL**	**80**	***71**	***125**	***196**	**59**	**16**	**12**	***26**	***38**	**4**
1983-84	**Edmonton Oilers**	**NHL**	**74**	***87**	***118**	***205**	**39**	**19**	**13**	***22**	***35**	**12**
1984-85	Team Canada	Can-Cup	8	5	7	12	2	....	....	....	....	....
	Edmonton Oilers	**NHL**	**80**	***73**	***135**	***208**	**52**	**18**	**17**	***30**	***47**	**4**
1985-86	**Edmonton Oilers**	**NHL**	**80**	**52**	***163**	***215**	**42**	**10**	**8**	**11**	**19**	**2**
1986-87	**Edmonton Oilers**	**NHL**	**79**	***62**	***121**	***183**	**28**	**21**	**5**	***29**	**34**	**6**
	NHL All-Stars	RV-87	2	0	4	4	0	....	....	....	....	....
1987-88	Team Canada	Can-Cup	9	3	*18	*21	2	....	....	....	....	....
	Edmonton Oilers	**NHL**	**64**	**40**	***109**	**149**	**24**	**19**	**12**	***31**	***43**	**16**
1988-89	**Los Angeles Kings**	**NHL**	**78**	**54**	***114**	**168**	**26**	**11**	**5**	**17**	**22**	**0**
1989-90	**Los Angeles Kings**	**NHL**	**73**	**40**	***102**	***142**	**42**	**7**	**3**	**7**	**10**	**0**
1990-91	**Los Angeles Kings**	**NHL**	**78**	**41**	***122**	***163**	**16**	**12**	**4**	**11**	**15**	**2**
1991-92	Team Canada	Can-Cup	7	4	8	12	2	....	....	....	....	....
	Los Angeles Kings	**NHL**	**74**	**31**	***90**	**121**	**34**	**6**	**2**	**5**	**7**	**2**
1992-93	**Los Angeles Kings**	**NHL**	**45**	**16**	**49**	**65**	**6**	**24**	***15**	***25**	***40**	**4**
1993-94	**Los Angeles Kings**	**NHL**	**81**	**38**	***92**	***130**	**20**	....	....	....	....	....
1994-95	**Los Angeles Kings**	**NHL**	**48**	**11**	**37**	**48**	**6**	....	....	....	....	....
1995-96	**Los Angeles Kings**	**NHL**	**62**	**15**	**66**	**81**	**32**	....	....	....	....	....
	St. Louis Blues	**NHL**	**18**	**8**	**13**	**21**	**2**	**13**	**2**	**14**	**16**	**0**
1996-97	Team Canada	W-Cup	6	3	4	7	2	....	....	....	....	....
	New York Rangers	**NHL**	**82**	**25**	***72**	**97**	**28**	**15**	**10**	**10**	**20**	**2**
1997-98	**New York Rangers**	**NHL**	**82**	**23**	***67**	**90**	**28**	....	....	....	....	....
	Team Canada	Olympics	6	0	4	4	2	....	....	....	....	....
1998-99	**New York Rangers**	**NHL**	**70**	**9**	**53**	**62**	**14**	....	....	....	....	....
NHL Totals	20 seasons	NHL	1487	*894	*1963	*2857	577	208	*122	*260	*382	66
WHA Totals	1 season	WHA	80	46	64	110	19	13	10	10	20	2
NHL/WHA Totals	21 seasons		1567	940	*2027	*2967	596	221	*132	*270	*402	68

* indicates League leader

HONOR ROLL

WJC All-Star Team (1978) • Best Forward WJC (1978) • OHA 2nd All-Star Team (1978) • WHA Second All-Star Team (1979) • Won Lou Kaplan Trophy (WHA Rookie-of-the Year) (1979) • Won Hart Trophy (1980, 1981, 1982, 1983, 1984, 1985, 1986, 1987, 1989) • Won Lady Byng Trophy (1980, 1991, 1992, 1994, 1999) • NHL Second All-Star Team (1980, 1988, 1989, 1990, 1994, 1997, 1998) • NHL First All-Star Team (1981, 1982, 1983, 1984, 1985, 1986, 1987, 1991) • Won Art Ross Trophy (1981, 1982, 1983, 1984, 1985, 1986, 1987, 1990, 1991, 1994) • Won Lester B. Pearson Award (1982, 1983, 1984, 1985, 1987) • WEC-A All-Star Team (1982) • Canada Cup All-Star Team (1984, 1987, 1991) • Won Conn Smythe Trophy (1985, 1988) • NHL Plus/Minus Leader (1982, 1984, 1985, 1987) • Won Lester Patrick Award (1994).

TRANSACTIONS AND MILESTONES

Sault Ste. Marie Greyhounds (OHA Jr. A) 1st choice, 3rd overall, in 1977 OHA Jr. A Priority Draft. • Signed as an underage free agent by **Indianapolis Racers** (WHA), June 12, 1978. • Traded to **Edmonton Oilers** (WHA) by **Indianapolis Racers** (WHA) with Eddie Mio and Peter Driscoll for cash, November 2, 1978. • Claimed by **Edmonton Oilers** as a Priority Selection in 1979 Expansion Draft, June 9, 1979. • Recorded point #153 of season vs. Pittsburgh to become NHL's single season points leader, March 29, 1981. • Scored goal #50 of season vs. Philadelphia in only 39 games to establish new NHL record for fastest 50 goals, December 30, 1981. • Scored goal #77 of season vs. Buffalo to become NHL's all-time leading single-season scorer, February 24, 1982. • Traded to **Los Angeles Kings** by **Edmonton Oilers** with Mike Krushelnyski and Marty McSorley for Jimmy Carson, Martin Gelinas, Los Angeles Kings' 1st round choice in 1989 (later acquired by New Jersey, who selected Jason Miller), 1991 (Martin Rucinsky) and 1993 (Nick Stajduhar) Entry Drafts and cash, August 9, 1988. • Recorded career point #1851 vs. Edmonton to become NHL's all-time leading scorer, October 15, 1989. • Traded to **St. Louis** by **Los Angeles Kings** for Craig Johnson, Patrice Tardif, Roman Vopat, St. Louis' 5th round choice (Peter Hogan) in 1996 Entry Draft and 1st round choice (Matt Zultek) in 1997 Entry Draft, February 27, 1996. • Scored career goal #802 vs. Vancouver to become NHL's all-time leading goal scorer, March 23, 1994. • Signed as a free agent by **New York Rangers**, July 21, 1996. • Officially announced retirement, April 16, 1999. • Recorded point #2857 of career vs. Pittsburgh, April 18, 1999.